THE WATER THAT DIVIDES

THE WATER THAT DIVIDES

Donald Bridge and David Phypers

Mentor

© Donald Bridge and David Phypers
ISBN 1 85792 252 2
This edition published in 1998 in the Mentor imprint
by
Christian Focus Publications,
Geanies House, Fearn, Ross-shire,
IV20 1TW, Great Britain.
Previously published in 1977
Printed by J W Arrowsmith Ltd., Bristol

Contents

Introduction

One of Jesus' last recorded commands to his followers was, 'Go... and make disciples of all nations, baptizing them in the name of the Father and of the Son and of the Holy Spirit' (Matt. 28:19). Most of his followers have obeyed his command. With the rare exception of groups like the Quakers and the Salvation Army, Christians of all traditions, denominations and persuasions have regarded baptism as the means of entry into the church. Yet despite this, perhaps no other command of Christ has occasioned so much controversy, division, bitterness and mutual mistrust. Christians have attacked each other, verbally and physically, with a ferocity strangely at variance with him who constantly exhorted his disciples to 'love one another' (John 15:12, 17).

Today, thankfully, the bitterest language has abated, and Christians rarely ill-treat each other over baptismal issues. Tolerance abounds. 'Best let sleeping dogs lie', seems to sum up the mood of most lay Christians, as they explore neighbourly relationships with believers of other traditions, via united Lenten services, area evangelistic missions and joint action against injustice. Meanwhile the professionals (theologians, bishops, ecumenical officers and the like) take an occasional cautious prod at the recumbent animals, only to find that dogs still bite. The corporate scars remain. Where there is peace of a kind, it is based more on a mixture of nervous defensiveness, misinformation or sheer boredom than on any godly consensus. And wherever there is life and progress in the churches (as increasingly there is, thanks be to God) the animals wake up and leap into action, in a disconcerting fashion.

Consider a few examples. Imagine a modern young man whose early religious pathway has been a typical one of baptism in infancy, sporadic attendance at Sunday school in childhood, and a tearless parting from the church in his teenage years in favour of the more alluring interests of motorcycle, girlfriend and disco. Then he meets vital Christianity for the first time. He is intrigued, impressed, troubled and eventually convinced. Christ becomes a reality. Life takes on new meaning. After a while he finds in baptism a rite tailor-made

to express his new convictions. But what is this? His vicar is horrified. His new Christian friends are embarrassed. A Baptist minister
down the road offers him baptism, or is it (whisper the word) rebaptism? Already, the Christian community which he was beginning
to like and trust appears to be divided. He must make a decision for
which he is ill-equipped, and which bewilderingly presents itself as a
matter of group loyalty. What is he to do?

Here is quite a different problem. Middle-aged parents with growing children move into a new area. They are life-long committed
Christians, used to taking pride in the fact that faith transcends denominational barriers. Bible conventions and evangelistic crusades,
youth camps and united Weeks of Prayer have all underlined this
fact, and, if truth be told, these parents are just a little bit derisive
about the 'ecumaniacs' who want to merge the denominations and
their structures. 'We already have spiritual unity! We are all one in
Christ Jesus!' they exclaim dismissively. But what is this? In their
new neighbourhood they look anxiously for a church that will honour
the Bible, proclaim the gospel in the power of the Holy Spirit, provide teaching and attractive fellowship for their offspring. The name
on the noticeboard matters little. Yet after finding such a church and
attending for some time, they ask for membership – and the difficulties begin! If they were baptized as infants and later confirmed the
Baptist church may demand that they be rebaptized in order to enjoy
the benefits and privileges of full membership. It is no longer enough
to welcome them as brother and sister in Christ. If, on the other hand,
they wish to enter fully into the life of the parish Church of England,
sooner or later they will find they need to be confirmed. To believe
and be baptized is not, apparently, enough after all.

A third example is common. Two Christians decide to marry. They
come from different denominational churches, but they met at college in the cheerfully eclectic atmosphere of the Christian Union.
Obviously they must settle for membership of one church, so one of
them graciously steps down and offers to join the other's denomination. Splendid! Unfortunately, the wife (let us say) who has taken the
humble place must now be humbled still further. Her husband, it seems,
was initiated the right way, but she got it wrong. She must retrace her
steps and be rebaptized or confirmed (whichever is required), contrary to her own convictions, for the sake of the family.

A fourth example is the saddest. The family are unabashed pagans, one and all. They hold the religion of the average Englishman; the belief that there may well be a God somewhere, but, as little is known about him, all that is required is to be as decent as the next man and kind to old ladies. A new baby arrives. Custom suggests (and grandmother insists) that something religious should be done. The vicar is called in. Presumably he sits in his vicarage waiting for little tasks like this, for that is his job. For a few precious moments the Christian church is touching the circle of interests of those it rarely reaches. But in the event, how pathetic is the occasion! The family stand apprehensively around the font at the back of an empty church. Hands are shaken with the vicar, and the party hurries home. Grandparents are satisfied, mother a little misty-eyed, father confirmed in his impression that religion has got nothing whatever to do with real life. Years later, if the growing child stumbles across some evangelistic activity and is prompted to ask, 'Mummy, am I a Christian?' he receives the indignant reply, 'Of course you are! You were baptized, weren't you?'

All of these sad stories illustrate the fact that controversy about baptism is far from being an academic luxury for armchair theologians. The witness of the church when it touches the unconverted, and the unity of the church when it welcomes the converted, are both at stake. In 1996, a newspaper columnist renowned for her tart but perceptive comments, attended a 'society' christening, and afterwards wondered aloud about the required qualifications of parents and godparents. In this particular case, she averred, they numbered 'two adulterers, a drunk and an international arms dealer'. An Anglican priest with a powerful evangelistic ministry has just shared with one of the authors of this book, the fact that after anxious study of the Bible (and of this book's first edition!), he had delayed the baptism of his own three children, and was awaiting the time when they would freely take that step of faith and commitment which he almost daily urged upon others. 'But of course I believe they belong to God,' he added.

Most recently built Roman Catholic and Anglican churches in Greater London have tiled baptisteries suitable for adult baptism by immersion. One parish church not so equipped swings an industrial skip through the double doorway and fills it with water; the bishop has let it be known that he would prefer not to hear about it. In a recent joint Anglican-Baptist mission conducted by one of the authors of this book, the problem of baptism and rebaptism never arose, for, as the vicar explained, no-one in that pagan area ever thought of bringing babies to be baptized. In what may be England's oldest city, a Greek Orthodox church has been established, and is crowded every week; its liturgy, of course, makes provision for the baptism of infants and adults by immersion.

We, the authors, have faced situations where one of two unmarried partners has become a Christian, the other still does not wish to marry, but they both agree that their children, born out of wedlock, should now begin to be brought up in the Christian faith. We have met mothers who now bitterly regret an abortion, and want to know how they may have some assurance as to the eternal fate of what they once called a foetus, but now see as a child. We could go on multiplying hair-raising examples of once unimagined implications of the baptismal debate.

We wrote the original edition of this book in 1977. We were friends who had worked together in the same 'closed membership' Baptist church; one as minister, the other as a deacon. Don had then moved on to pastor a large 'open membership' church which taught baptism for believers only, but did not require it for membership. Meanwhile David had begun training for the Anglican ministry, and had perforce to re-examine his beliefs and priorities. Both of us were deeply involved in evangelism, church growth and renewal. Fascinating though we found theology and history to be, our most urgent attention was directed to winning new disciples for Christ and his church, in an age of rapidly growing secularism and paganism. Our correspondence and heart-sharing led to the book being written.

It was well received, translated into Dutch, and published in the United States of America. Over the years we have often been urged to update and reprint it, and until that was possible many colleges, libraries and local churches have asked permission to photocopy the first edition. Now the original publishers, Inter-Varsity Press, have kindly agreed that Christian Focus should print a completely rewritten and updated book.

The rewriting has had to be more extensive than we first anticipated, and only four historical chapters remain almost unaltered. Events have moved on, in two decades of dramatic change within and without the churches. We can list some of them: church unity schemes, charismatic renewal, the growth of 'restoration churches', liturgical reform, the planting of thousands of new churches in what was once thought of as 'the mission-field', the pervasiveness of postmodern attitudes which devalue doctrine and logic but value experience and symbol. All of these factors focus attention on the great baptismal questions. What is the meaning and purpose of baptism? Who should be baptized, and how should it be administered? Does anything actually *happen* in baptism? Why do Christians disagree on so basic an issue? Are differences of opinion sufficient to threaten our basic oneness as Christians? Can we afford to spend energy on point-scoring, when a world is dying without Christ?

We make no claim to resolve the issues which have divided Christians for two thousand years. But we believe that Christians should face these issues fairly and squarely. We should learn to live together in understanding rather than in ignorance.

Hence we begin by looking at New Testament references to Christian baptism and drawing conclusions from them. Next we concentrate on elucidating the reasons why some Christians believe that adult converts and their children should be baptized, while others are willing to baptize adult converts only.

Thirdly, we show how these questions arose at various times in history, and were never a matter of pure theology. Rather, they were thrown up by cultural, emotional, religious and political factors. To use a postmodern phrase, a living 'text' (biblical teaching about baptism) took on various lives, and became 'styled' in radically different ways at different times. The question, How can I follow Christ today? became rightly and inevitably entangled in questions like, Who do I perceive myself to be?, In what kind of society do I live?, What does Christian discipleship have to say, in judgment and in hope, to that society?

Finally, we look at the situation today, sum up the new issues raised as the church confronts rampant paganism in a pluralistic age, and make practical suggestions whereby Christians might succeed in worshipping and working together without surrendering cherished beliefs and practices.

Throughout the book the word 'paedobaptist' will be used to describe those who accept the validity and necessity of baptizing infants and little children incapable of conscious faith. The word 'baptist' (with a small 'b') will describe all others who insist on the need for conscious faith to precede baptism. Such baptists are not necessarily adult baptists, so we have usually avoided that phrase. Not all baptists are Baptists (with a capital 'B'); baptist belief extends far beyond specifically named Baptist churches and denominations. In recent years the word 'baptistic' has come into increasing use, but we have used it here only sparingly.

Part 1

Baptism and Scripture

1

Baptism in the New Testament

The reader of the New Testament is confronted immediately with baptism. To avoid it, one would have to ignore the events surrounding the beginning of Christ's ministry and the start of the church's life. For the first public appearance of Jesus was heralded by John's baptism, the first public act of Jesus was to be baptized, and the first evangelistic sermon of the infant church was climaxed by a mass-baptism.

These facts raise immediate questions to which scholars have given much attention. How much was John's baptism borrowed from popular Jewish customs? Why did Jesus submit to baptism? How much development was there between the simple rite recorded in Acts and the theological significance given to it in Paul's epistles? A full enquiry is quite beyond the scope of this book,[1] but every Christian should at least be aware of the more obvious scriptural references.

The baptism of John

Mark's Gospel gives us the fullest account of the significance of John's baptism, while some additional material is provided by the other Evangelists. First, says Mark, 'John the baptizer appeared in the wilderness, preaching a baptism of repentance....' (Mark 1:4). People who came to John for baptism therefore needed to be conscious of failure and of guilt. They had to be sufficiently concerned about it to abandon certain kinds of behaviour. They had to show a practical desire for a better way of life. Significantly, John's most scathing words were reserved for those who sought his baptism without fulfilling these conditions. The Pharisees and Sadducees (religious and political leaders of the Jews) were told to 'bear fruit that befits repentance' (Matt. 3:8). The enthusiastic crowds in general were warned that more was involved than a moving ceremony and some revivalist excitement: selfishness should give way to generosity, dishonesty to fairness, bullying to kindness and grumbling to gratitude (see Luke 3:7-14).

15

Secondly, John's message spoke of what God gives as well as what he demands. Those who were baptized not only expressed their sorrow for past misdeeds, but also echoed their joyful discovery that God was willing to wipe the slate clean. So, as they confessed their sins (Mark 1:5), they looked backward to failure, forward to amendment, and upward for forgiveness. These elements of confession, repentance and forgiveness were the main features of John's baptism as described in Mark's account.

Matthew, however, tells us more. John's baptism had an eschatological dimension. It was concerned with 'the last days', with a turning point in history, with a climactic moment in God's dealings with mankind. It was because the kingdom of heaven was 'at hand' that John issued his call (Matt. 3:2). It was from 'the wrath to come' that people needed to flee (Matt. 3:7). 'Even now,' said John, 'the axe is laid to the root of the trees' (Matt. 3:10). For this reason the people must repent and be baptized.

The Christian reader, wise after the event, can see how right John was. A unimaginable crisis was at hand. All human history had been moving towards this moment. The purpose hidden in God's heart before creation was about to be unfolded. The Christ who was God's unique provision and mankind's only hope, was about to burst upon the scene. Individuals' reaction to these events would reveal their inmost motives and either condemn them or bring them in to the sweep of God's plan. Nothing would ever be the same again!

For this reason, all the Evangelists agree that John's baptism was preparatory and incomplete. John himself acknowledged this. 'I baptize you with water for repentance,' he proclaimed, 'but he who is coming after me.... will baptize you with the Holy Spirit and with fire' (Matt. 3:11; see also Mark 1:8; Luke 3:16; John 1:33). The people needed John's baptism, they needed to confess and repent of their sins, they needed to accept God's forgiveness, but when they had done all this they must not think that God had no more to offer or demand. John's baptism was but a preparation for another baptism; one of immersion in the life of the Holy Spirit. Only the Coming One would give that!

Jewish precedents

Behind John's mission stood the whole Jewish tradition. Water has always been a potent religious symbol. Rivers ran out of Eden (Gen. 2:10), ritual washings were regular at the desert tabernacle (Lev. 15:1-6), and another river ran from beneath the Temple in Ezekiel's vision (Ezek. 47:1-12). Here are double concepts of life and cleansing.

Stories gripped Jewish imagination too: the flood water that separated Noah from a godless generation, the stream that flowed from the rock struck by Moses, and Naaman's seven plunges in the River Jordan to cleanse his leprosy (Gen. 7:1-4; Exod. 17:1-7; and 2 Kings 5:1-14). These also carried the same double meaning.

In the two centuries preceding and following the birth of Jesus, proselyte baptism was widely practised. It marked entry to the Jewish Covenant for those born among pagan Gentiles who were later drawn to faith in the one, true living God. This washing ceremony was added to circumcision to cover the ceremonial impurity suffered before conversion. Candidates were questioned about their motives, told some of the laws they would have to observe, and, if they consented, were circumcised immediately. When healed, they immersed themselves naked, or, in the case of women, were put in the water by other women.[2]

Recent archaeological and literary research has also shown how repeated immersions had become part of pious Jewish life by the time of John the Baptist. Excavations since 1970 have uncovered over a hundred stepped ritual pools in the old city of Jerusalem, and three times as many more throughout Judaea. Frequently mentioned in the rabbinical writings, these *mikva'ot* had dimensions exactly prescribed. The preference was for 'living (running) water'. To facilitate this in a static pool there was an adjoining smaller container, an *otzar*, from which stored water could be released into the larger pool at the moment of immersion.[3] These ritual pools were for wealthier Jews to mark personal religious and domestic events.

Evidence from Qumran, where the Dead Sea Scrolls were discovered in 1947, has revealed other intriguing customs which provide parallels if not precedents for Jewish baptism. The earnest Essene sectarians who lived in this remote desert community and also in the south-western quarter of Jerusalem were immersed at least once every day! Their expectations focused on a new 'living temple' that the promised Messiah would build with those who gave themselves totally to obedience to God. One of their favourite proof texts was precisely that vision from Isaiah 40, of the Voice in the Wilderness, which John the Baptizer made his own.

Jesus' baptism

Against this background of custom (the *mitva'ot*) and innovation (John's baptism of repentance), Jesus came to John for baptism (see Matt. 3:13-17; Mark 1:9-11; Luke 3:21-22; John 1:29-34). But why? He had no sins to confess (Heb. 4:15). His only reply to the reformer's hesitation was the enigmatic, 'Let it be so now; for thus it is fitting for us to fulfil all righteousness' (Matt. 3:15). What did that mean? May it be paraphrased simply as, 'It is always right to do the right thing'? Christian reflection (and indeed biblical comment) has seen much more.[4]

For example, the word-picture in Isaiah 53 depicts a suffering Messiah, 'despised and rejected.... wounded for our transgressions' (verses 3-5). Identifying this vision with Jesus the Christ, the writer to the Hebrews describes his partaking of our human nature, feeling our pressures and temptations, being like his brothers in every respect, helping those who are tempted because he has suffered but not yielded (Heb. 2:14-18). In other words, here is Christ's total identification with humankind as he takes his place alongside sinners, becoming, to the casual observer at least, completely indistinguishable from them.

This Jesus consistently did, and was often misunderstood as a result. To people who equated religion with a strict separation from certain open misdeeds and a critical attitude towards the less scrupulous, the relationship of Jesus with all kinds of people, particularly those marginalized by religion, was a continual puzzle. He did not seem to be particular about the company he kept; he seemed to like joining in parties; he offered friendship to undesirable characters; he clothed religious conceptions in shockingly homely speech. He sat loose to the many regulations that normally pushed a devout person out of the company of others. 'This man receives sinners and eats with them,' they complained (Luke 15:2).

Misunderstanding was inevitable, for, to some, a person is judged by the company he keeps. Indeed, to the rabbinical establishment, the company one kept precisely defined whether one was, or was not, a true member of God's Special People. Yet to a ministry marked by the attitude of Jesus, acceptance of John's baptism was a suitable prelude, for in that baptism he was associating himself with sinners. More than that, he was identifying himself with their situation. So complete was that identification that its climax was reached in his death when, hanging between two thieves on a cross prepared for a third, 'he himself bore our sins in his body on the tree' (1 Pet. 2:24).

How then did Jesus' baptism 'fulfil all righteousness'? Righteousness was a technical term in the Jewish world of Jesus' day. It denoted both the righteous demands of God on humankind, and the righteous intervention of God in saving those who cry to him. For Jesus, in particular, that meant accepting the task of providing salvation for those who turn to God. By insisting on baptism at the hands of John, Jesus was taking a decisive step of submission and humiliation in a process that began at Bethlehem and was to end at Calvary, in obedience to the Father's will. How appropriate, then, that that obedience should be recognized by his Father; that 'when he came up out of the water, immediately he saw the heavens opened and the Spirit descending upon him like a dove; and a voice came from heaven, "Thou art my beloved Son; with thee I am well pleased"' (Mark 1:10-11)! So Jesus' Messianic work began. The Spirit was given to aid him in his task, while the Father testified his good pleasure in him who 'did not count equality with God a thing to be grasped, but emptied himself...' (Phil. 2:6-7).

However, the extent to which we can identify Christ's baptism with Christian baptism is limited. Jesus was (and is) unique. What his baptism meant to him in terms of the kingdom coming in his person, and in terms of his personal awareness of Sonship, has parallels but not equivalents with us. The oft-repeated baptist exhortation to 'follow your Lord in baptism' can mean no more than 'obey, just as he obeyed'. What his obedience meant to him is not what our obedience means to us.

Christian baptism

Christian baptism was first administered on the Day of Pentecost and its similarity to John's baptism is immediately apparent. 'Repent, and be baptized,' commanded Peter when his audience was 'cut to the heart' (Acts 2:37-38). 'Be baptized... in the name of Jesus Christ for the forgiveness of your sins,' he continued (Acts 2:38). Thus far there is little difference in his message from John's. Christian baptism, like John's baptism, is both a sign and a vehicle of repentance and forgiveness. But more; John had foreseen and foretold baptism in the Holy Spirit, and this Peter now promised to his hearers. 'Repent ... and be baptized ... and you shall receive the gift of the Holy Spirit' (Acts 2:38).

This connection between water-baptism and Spirit-baptism recurs throughout the Acts of the Apostles. Ananias went to see Saul in Damascus that he might regain his sight and be filled with the Holy Spirit. And after Saul had regained his sight 'he rose and was baptized' (Acts 9:17-18). At the house of Cornelius, after the Holy Spirit had been poured out, Peter declared, '"Can any one forbid water for baptizing these people who have received the Holy Spirit just as we have?" And he commanded them to be baptized' (Acts 10:45-48). Yet again, after baptizing the twelve men at Ephesus, Paul laid hands on them and the Holy Spirit came upon them (see Acts 19:5-6).

The same connection is made in the epistles. 'For by one Spirit we were all baptized into one body,' writes Paul, 'and all were made to drink of one Spirit' (1 Cor. 12:13). Again, in his letter to Titus he speaks in the same breath of 'the washing of regeneration and renewal in the Holy Spirit' (see Titus 3:5-7). Besides these explicit references, many scholars believe that when Paul speaks of 'the seal of the Spirit' (see, for example, 2 Cor. 1:22; Eph. 1:13; 4:30) he is referring to his readers' water-baptism.[5]

This direct equation between baptism and reception of the Holy Spirit cannot be stressed too strongly. Throughout Christian history many have separated the two, using the idea of a later experience of a baptism in the Spirit to justify the practice of confirmation. In the present century pentecostal and charismatic teaching has made a similar separation on rather different grounds. Yet, to put it mildly, such a separation is hard to justify in purely New Testament terms. Admittedly, water-baptism and Spirit-baptism are logically separate events, and each is possible without the other. The Samaritans in Acts 8 were baptized in water without being baptized in the Spirit. The Romans in Acts 10 were baptized in the Spirit without being baptized in water. But theologically the two belong together. They are different aspects of one great initiation complex that includes the inward attitudes of repentance and faith, the outward marks of water-baptism and the laying-on of hands, and the declaration by God of sin's forgiveness and heart renewal. The subjective enjoyment of these things may well be delayed or disconnected. It is possible to be forgiven and not to feel clean. It is possible to be inwardly renewed and yet not to be joyfully and liberatingly conscious of it. It is possible to be incompletely aware of what God has given, or to be aware of it but to neglect it. It is possible to be ill-instructed about God's gifts, or emotionally unable to enjoy them fully. Yet since the Day of Pentecost to which John pointed, there is no need deliberately to separate water-baptism and Spirit-baptism, nor does the New Testament do this.

Baptism in the New Testament also demonstrates that salvation is all of God's grace. Writing to Titus, Paul declares, 'when the goodness and loving kindness of God our Saviour appeared, he saved us, not because of deeds done by us in righteousness, but in virtue of his own mercy, by the washing of regeneration...' (Titus 3:4-5). Grace is fundamental in the New Testament. It speaks of the favour and kindness which God extends to men and women utterly regardless of their condition or their deserts. It can never be said too strongly that God's love for us has nothing at all to do with our being loveable or even likeable. His love for a depraved and disgusting renegade whom he is calling back to himself is the same in quantity and quality as his love for a newborn baby who has had no opportunity to break human or divine laws. This is very hard for human beings to grasp, because however much we use the word grace, in fact we cannot break free from ideas of love that connect it with merit and approval. Persistently we fall back on the hope of earning God's grace and of putting him in our debt, forgetting that such expressions are a contradiction in terms. So one will seek to grasp God's love and salvation by moral earnestness, another by religious observance, another by sensibly 'deciding for Christ'. But 'by grace you have been saved through faith; and this is not your own doing, it is the gift of God' (Eph. 2:8). Because baptism is a declaration of the gospel, it is an announcement of God's grace: the emphasis, as in Paul's words to Titus, is on God's coming to us, not on our doing something for him.

This gracious salvation is appropriated by faith, and baptism declares this too. When the Samaritans believed Philip as he preached good news about the kingdom of God and the name of Jesus Christ, they were baptized (Acts 8:12). When the Ethiopian eunuch asked Philip, 'What is to prevent my being baptized?', an early addition to the text of Acts, regarded as authentic by many New Testament scholars, tells us that Philip replied, 'If you believe with all your heart, you may.' And the eunuch replied, 'I believe that Jesus Christ is the Son of God.' Then Philip baptized him (see Acts 8:36-38 with footnote). When the Philippian gaoler asked Paul and Silas, 'What must I do to be saved?' Paul replied, 'Believe in the Lord Jesus, and you will be saved, you and your household.' And he was baptized at once, with all his family (see Acts 16:30-33). When Paul preached in Corinth, 'many of the Corinthians hearing Paul believed and were baptized' (Acts 18:8). And when Paul wrote to the Colossians he declared, 'you were buried with him in baptism, in which you were also raised with him through faith in the working of God...' (Col. 2:12). In the New Testament faith and baptism are always intimately connected, each being held to complement the other.

New Testament teaching also stresses the connection between baptism and the Christian's participation in the death and resurrection of Christ (see Rom. 6:1-4; Col. 2:12ff.). Coming to Christ involves dying and rising with him, and there is no more vivid reminder of this than the act of baptism itself. Entering the water the Christian shares in Christ's death ('we were buried... with him by baptism unto death', Rom. 6:4; 'you were buried with him in baptism', Col. 2:12): leaving the water he shares in his resurrection ('in which you were also raised with him', Col. 2:12). In dying with Christ the Christian dies to sin. He accepts God's forgiveness secured on the cross (see Col. 2:14) and his old self is crucified with Christ that his sinful body might be destroyed and he might no longer be enslaved to sin (see Rom. 6:6). In rising with Christ the Christian becomes alive to God (Rom. 6:11). The life he henceforth lives he lives to God (Rom. 6:10). Death and sin no longer have dominion over him (see Rom. 6:9, 14).

This fundamental change from death to life, which occurs in a person's life when he comes to Christ, is called elsewhere in the New Testament, 'being born anew' (see John 3; 1 Pet. 1:3) and its representation in baptism causes Paul to speak of 'the washing of regeneration and renewal' (Tit. 3:5). While the New Testament insists that regeneration must involve a personal response to the claims of Christ, it also makes clear that, having been born anew, the Christian cannot and must not continue to live in isolation from others, for once regenerate, the Christian becomes a member of the people of God, the church. Thus, baptism in the New Testament is portrayed as the means of entry into the Christian church. Paul writes, 'by one Spirit we were all baptized into one body' (1 Cor. 12:13). To be baptized without belonging to the church is a contradiction in New Testament terms. The three thousand who were baptized on the Day of Pentecost, 'devoted themselves to the apostles' teaching and fellowship, to the breaking of bread and the prayers' (Acts 2:42), and these were corporate not individual activities.

Finally, like John's baptism, Christian baptism in the New Testament has an eschatological dimension. It is concerned with the last days. Paul speaks of 'the washing of regeneration... so that we might... become heirs... of eternal life' (Titus 3:5-7). Those who are baptized look to the future. Already alive to God, they see beyond the grave to the perfect life when they will live and reign with Christ for ever.

Immersion, pouring or sprinkling?

Tantalizingly, for all the rich symbolism with which the New Testament writers surround baptism, they nowhere tell us how to do it, or even how it was done when they relate it! Yet Christians have differed passionately on this issue, even denying the validity of baptism when, in their view, it has not been performed correctly. Immersion, pouring and sprinkling are the three ways in which water has been used, and still is, among Christians worldwide.

The meaning of the Greek verb *baptizein*, 'to immerse', and the burial and resurrection symbolism of Romans 6 and Colossians 2, give powerful theological support to the claim that baptism by immersion was normal in the early church. But was it? Peter's first letter, regarded by many scholars as a baptismal treatise, is addressed to 'exiles ... chosen and destined by God the Father and sanctified by the Spirit for obedience to Jesus Christ and for sprinkling with his blood' (1 Pet. 1:2). The writer to the Hebrews also refers to the 'sprinkled blood' of Jesus that 'speaks more graciously than the blood of Abel' (Heb. 12:24). Might these references not suggest that the recipients of both letters had been sprinkled with water rather than immersed when they had been baptized?

When Peter went to preach in the home of Cornelius he baptized his hearers when the Holy Spirit was 'poured out' on them (Acts 10:45). Quite apart from the symbolism, baptism by pouring (or affusion) seems to fit the tone of the narrative much more comfortably than immersion, if only for practical reasons. Indeed, this can be said about most of the baptisms described in the Acts of the Apostles.

Sceptical scholars long denied the historical accuracy of the Day of Pentecost narrative (Acts 3) on the grounds that sufficient water would not have been available to the apostles to baptize three thousand people in the forecourts of the Temple. However, recent discovery of at least twenty ritual baths in the houses near the Temple's southern staircase, and further discovery that the Old City had (and still has) a huge number of underground cisterns to collect and store rainwater, often with easy access by carved staircases, have answered that objection.

The story of the baptism of the Philippian gaoler and his family raises similar questions. Does it really imply that the entire household, together with Paul and Silas bleeding from their flogging, trooped through the streets to the river in the early hours of the morning, in the aftermath of an earthquake, in order for the penitents to be immersed? The only water actually mentioned in the story is the few basinfuls used to wash the evangelists' wounds; the appropriateness of baptism by effusion with the same water is rather appealing, if somewhat melodramatic!

Baptisms by immersion there clearly were in the New Testament, and possibly they were the most common. The Ethiopian eunuch was almost certainly immersed, for we read that both he and Philip 'went down into the water' and 'came up out of the water' (Acts 8:38-39). Lydia and her household were probably immersed, for Paul preached to them by the riverside (Acts 16:12-15). And later, Paul drew lessons from the symbolic 'burial' of immersion, as has been seen. But equally he drew lessons from the symbolic 'putting off' of the candidates' old clothes and the 'putting on' of baptismal garments, in what are generally regarded as baptismal passages (Rom. 13:12-14; Col. 3:8-14). Yet it would be a rash person indeed who argued that a baptism was not valid if it was not preceded by undressing and dressing in order to provide the symbol. An insistence on the precise detailed copying of the symbol lays the emphasis in the wrong place. Is the symbol more important than the reality? Does the outward take precedence over the inward? Such an attitude ill accords with the spirit of the gospel.

Certainly there is no reason why baptism should be delayed or abandoned because facilities for immersion are not available, or because delicacy, infirmity or old age make it inadvisable. Nor should Christians be made to feel that their own baptism is invalid or inferior merely because of the small amount of water used. While we respect deeply held convictions about the mode of baptism, we would like to hope that, at the end of the twentieth century, Christians can stop quarrelling about this issue where baptism of adults is concerned. Where children are involved the issues are more serious and the division lines run more deeply.

References

1. For an excellent account of the issues involved see George Beasley-Murray, *Baptism in the New Testament* (Macmillan, 1963), chapters 1-4.
2. See Cheslyn Jones (ed.), *The Study of Liturgy*, (SPCK, 1992), page 73.
3. See *Biblical Archaeology Review*, Washington DC, Jan-Feb 1987, May-June 1992 and March-April 1993. The title of the first article is significant: *What Jewish Mikva'ot can tell us about Christian Baptism.*
4. See Beasley-Murray, *ibid*, pp. 45-46 for a valuable discussion.
5. See, for example, G. W. H. Lampe, *The Seal of the Spirit* (SPCK, 1967).

2

The Paedobaptist Approach

Kumar was a student at university in the north of England. Brought up in East Africa as a Hindu, he was deeply impressed by members of his college Christian Union, and quietly committed his life to Christ. Before long he saw the need to be baptized. Even though he knew that this public profession of faith would bring upon him the grief and anger of his family, he determined to claim 'his high allegiance'.

Few Christians would doubt he acted correctly, though the cost was high. For all agree that when an adult unbeliever or a member of any non-Christian religion is converted to Christ he should be baptized. On every continent, among Christians of every denomination, the baptism of such converts is a familiar and joyful sight. What is in dispute is the assertion that infants and little children should also be baptized.

Some Christians would say that all infants (or as many as possible) should be baptized, others would restrict baptism to the infants of parents who request their baptism, while others would limit baptism to the infants of practising Christians. Discounting, for the moment, these differences of opinion about the extent of paedobaptism, what reasons do these Christians advance to justify their position?

Historical evidence

a. The evidence of the Bible
There is no direct reference to paedobaptism in the New Testament itself. Nevertheless many affirm that it was practised because we read of several occasions when whole families and households were baptized. When Lydia was converted 'she was baptized, with her household' (Acts 16:15). When the Philippian gaoler heard the word of the Lord 'he was baptized at once, with all his family' (Acts 16:33). When Paul wrote to the Corinthians he recalled that he had baptized 'the household of Stephanas' (1 Cor. 1:16).

Now, say paedobaptists, it is inconceivable that in all these households there were no little children and infants. When their parents and other responsible members of the household were baptized the children were obviously included as well. This was how first-century Greek and Roman families operated; they were much more closely knit than their modern counterparts in Western society. Decisions made by the head of a family directly and almost unquestioningly affected all its members. Such households as Cornelius' (Acts 11:14), Crispus' (Acts 18:8) and Onesiphorus' (2 Tim. 1:16) provide examples of this principle in action. Thus, even if there were no infants at all in the families whose baptisms are actually recorded in the New Testament, infants born later into these families would automatically have been baptized at birth, or shortly afterwards. So, it is concluded, paedobaptism is a thoroughly scriptural practice.

b. The evidence of the Fathers

Soon after the beginning of the third century, Origen, the greatest scholar in the early church, declared: 'The Church has received a tradition from the Apostles to give baptism even to little children'.[1] Clearly he believed this; presumably he himself had been baptized as an infant. Had his parents in turn? And his grandparents? So suggests the modern German scholar Joachim Jeremias.[2] If he is correct, it follows that paedobaptism was being practised at least as early as the beginning of the second century, very close to the New Testament period.

The example of Polycarp is even more impressive. In 156 persecution broke out against Christians in Asia Minor. Among those who died for their faith was the aged Polycarp, bishop of Smyrna. His death, dramatic and moving, marked a watershed in the history of the early church. He was its last living link with the apostles themselves, having been influenced by John. Paraded in the stadium and commanded to curse Christ, he gave the noble reply, 'Eighty-six years have I served him, and he has done me no wrong: how then can I blaspheme my King who saved me?'[3] Must he not be referring to his infant baptism eighty-six years previously? Does not this imply that such baptism was therefore an apostolic practice?[4]

Similarly, Justin Martyr, who brilliantly defended Christianity in the second century like C. S. Lewis in the twentieth, referred to 'many men and women of the age of sixty and seventy years who have been disciples (or "were made disciples") of Christ from childhood'.[5] So here again (for those who seek it) is further evidence for childhood discipleship, and, by implication, paedobaptism, in late apostolic times.

c. The evidence of Jewish proselyte baptism

We have already seen how converts from paganism were baptized as well as circumcised when they embraced the Jewish faith.[6] We have also seen how many modern scholars believe that Christian baptism, as it developed, was influenced by Jewish baptism. Yet other scholars believe that children of converts to Judaism were sometimes baptized along with their parents. If they were, then children of Christian parents would naturally have been baptized, along with their parents, in the early church.

Particularly significant here are Paul's words of encouragement to Christians at Corinth who were married to non-Christians: 'For the unbelieving husband is consecrated through his wife, and the unbelieving wife is consecrated through her husband. Otherwise, your children would be unclean, but as it is they are holy' (1 Cor. 7:14). What does he mean? Is he reflecting the Jewish idea that children born to pagans before conversion to Judaism were 'born unclean', while those born after conversion were 'born in holiness'? Was this the reason, then, why children were baptized along with their parents, to make them 'clean' where they were 'unclean' before? Were the children of the Corinthian Christians, therefore, baptized for the same reason, when their parents were converted to Christ? If they were, then here is further impressive evidence for paedobaptism in at least one New Testament church. And the evidence is theological rather than sociological.

Theological evidence

a. The nature of baptism itself

We have already shown how the very first proclamation of the Christian gospel on the Day of Pentecost included a call to 'repent, and be baptized ... for the forgiveness of your sins ... For the promise is to you and to your children...' (Acts 2:38-39). From the beginning, Christians have understood a clear connection between baptism and forgiveness. 'Baptism ... now saves you ... as an appeal to God for a clear conscience' (1 Pet. 3:21). And from the beginning they have understood that their children need forgiveness just as much as themselves. Paul writes: 'Sin came into the world through one man and death through sin, and so death spread to all men because all men sinned' (Rom. 5:12).

If children are 'conceived in sin' (Psalm 51:5), and if baptism secures forgiveness of sin, then surely children should be baptized, and the sooner the better! In chapter 4 we shall show how the early Christians first justified paedobaptism from the idea of inherited sin, and then justified the idea of original sin from the practice of paedobaptism! Suffice to say, as in *The Baptism of Children* in the Church of England's *Alternative Service Book 1980*, a clear connection between baptism and forgiveness is maintained:

> Bless this water, that your servants who are washed in it may be made one with Christ in his death and in his resurrection, to be cleansed and delivered from all sin. Send your Holy Spirit upon them to bring them to new birth in the family of your Church, and raise them with Christ to full and eternal life.[7]

This raises big questions, particularly for Protestant and evangelical Christians who believe in the primacy of faith as the means of salvation. To these questions we shall, in due course, return.

b. Jesus and children
If the doctrine of original sin and the nature of baptism itself is held to support the baptism of infants, Jesus' teaching about children, as recorded in the Gospels, is also used to support the practice.

In Mark 10:13-16 we read:

> And they were bringing children to him, that he might touch them; and the disciples rebuked them. But when Jesus saw it he was indignant, and said to them, 'Let the children come to me, do not hinder them; for to such belongs the kingdom of God. Truly, I say to you, whoever does not receive the kingdom of God like a child shall not enter it.' And he took them in his arms and blessed them, laying his hands upon them.'

Parallel passages are found in Matthew 18:3; 19:13-15 and Luke 18:15-17. The Lukan version is particularly significant, for it makes the point that some, if not all, of the children who were brought to Jesus were 'even infants'; a different Greek word is used to describe them from the one translated 'children' in Matthew and Mark.

Admittedly, the reasoning goes, these passages are not concerned explicitly with baptism, but nonetheless they make paedobaptism imperative. Jesus was indignant with his disciples when they tried to turn the children away. Therefore, baptists who refuse baptism to little children are as guilty as the disciples. Jesus said that the kingdom of God belongs to children. He also said that the proper way for an adult to receive the kingdom is to become like the child. If the kingdom of God belongs to children, and if the way to receive the kingdom is to receive it as a child, how dare we refuse children, even infants, the sign of the kingdom, namely baptism? Jesus did not baptize the children who were brought to him because he did not baptize, and in any case Christian baptism had not been instituted. But by laying his hands on them Jesus showed that none of the blessings of the kingdom were to be denied to children, not even baptism.

c. Baptism and salvation

For many, the teaching and example of Jesus in the Gospels is sufficient justification for paedobaptism. Others, however, find further support for paedobaptism in scriptural teaching on the nature of salvation and the grace of God.

Salvation, they say, is the work of God. It is an objective thing, begun, enacted and finished solely by God himself. It does not depend on the subjective response of man in faith, for that response, though necessary, is itself part of God's work. To argue otherwise would be to make the response itself a 'work' which earns salvation. It is easy to reject the idea that salvation comes by self-effort, human decency or religious observance, and then slip into the suggestion that people are saved because they are sensitive enough or wise enough to respond to the offer of the gospel.

Because salvation is objective, the reasoning goes, adult baptism tends to emphasise the subjective response of the convert rather than the objective fact of God's grace. Paedobaptism, on the other hand, given to those who cannot exercise conscious faith, more aptly portrays the objective nature of salvation. So paedobaptism displays the prevenient grace of God. That is to say, God comes to us before we turn to him, as Jesus said to his disciples, 'You did not choose me, but I chose you...' (John 15:16). Oscar Cullmann has developed this idea in his book, *Baptism in the New Testament*. He sees the baptism of Christ as being the prototype of all subsequent Christian baptisms. When one is baptized one enters in to the baptism of Christ. Thus all the benefits of Christ's baptism were in a special sense prevenient. Because the infant who is baptized enjoys all the benefits of his baptism after he has been baptized, paedobaptism is a particularly suitable vehicle to display this aspect of baptism.

Cullmann's ideas have found expression in official Church of Scotland reports in recent years:

> 'Baptism' refers to the one all-inclusive, vicarious baptism of Christ for all men; the once-and-for-all baptism of Christ in blood upon the cross and the once-and-for-all baptism of the church in Spirit at Pentecost are correlative, and so the baptism of Christ for all men can be spoken of as the baptism of the church.... When an individual is baptized within this church, he too is baptized into Christ who was born of the Spirit, who died and who rose again. That is why the baptism of children of Christian parents is so right that it is taken for granted in the New Testament.[8]

Also

> Common humanity is shared by every man and by Christ Himself... the one qualification for baptism is [man's] membership in the sinful humanity which Christ has redeemed.[9]

Infants, just as much as adults, possess this qualification and thus should be baptized.

d. Baptism and the covenant of grace

Perhaps the most persuasive scriptural argument for paedobaptism is based on an understanding of the covenant of grace. It is an argument little understood by many who reject paedobaptism. Neither are its conclusions fully acceptable to all paedobaptists. Indeed, the line of reasoning is mainly found in the Scottish and continental Reformed churches and their overseas offshoots which find their inspiration in the teachings of John Knox and John Calvin. French Reformed pastor Pierre Ch Marcel has eloquently re-stated the position in recent times with his boldly entitled work, *The Biblical Doctrine of Infant Baptism*. Since the translation of his book into English in 1953 his views have been enthusiastically adopted by a growing number of evangelical Anglicans. Whatever the strength of the position, it was quite unknown before the Reformation and cannot be found in any form in any of the writings of the early Fathers. To its supporters this merely demonstrates how quickly New Testament teaching on the subject was lost in the Graeco-Roman world of the early Christian era.

(i) Two covenants or one?

What then is the basis of this covenant teaching? The Bible is divided into two main sections, the Old Testament and the New Testament. Some translations call these sections, quite correctly, the Old Covenant and the New Covenant, for in this context the words testament and covenant are synonymous. A covenant is a solemn, binding agreement with promises and obligations, entered into by two or more parties and often ratified by oaths and visible signs such as sacrifices and the exchange of tokens. Marriage is a good modern example of such a covenant. Two parties, the man and the woman, enter into a binding agreement with each other to live together as husband and wife. They make promises and accept obligations. Their agreement is ratified by the exchange of a ring or rings as visible tokens that the covenant has been properly entered into and will be observed.

Because the Bible is divided into the Old Covenant and the New Covenant it is commonly believed that it tells how God has made two covenants with humankind. The first covenant was concluded on Mount Sinai through Moses with the people of Israel (see Exodus 19–20). In it God offered salvation in return for obedience to his law. This 'old covenant' was thus the covenant of law. The second covenant, the 'new covenant', was concluded at Calvary with all humanity through Christ. In it God offers salvation in return for faith in Christ as the mediator of the covenant. This is the covenant of grace, through which the undeserved favour of God delivers men and women from the obligations of the covenant of law which were too difficult for them to keep anyway, and offers them salvation through faith in the sacrifice of Christ.

Supporters of covenant theology reject this common belief in two basic covenants. They affirm one covenant of grace, found throughout Old and New Testaments and always received by faith. The two halves of the Bible do not describe separate covenants made by God with humankind, but the way in which one covenant was administered differently, for necessary reasons.

In the Old Testament, God made his covenant with Abraham (Gen. 15:5) and renewed it at various times in his life. '[Abraham] believed the LORD; and he [God] reckoned it to him as righteousness' (Gen. 15:6). This is the covenant of grace and is referred to frequently in the New Testament. For example, in Romans Paul gives a careful reply to Jewish opponents of the gospel of grace. They quoted Abraham, their forefather, as a supreme example of justification by works. This is how God has acted from the beginning, they claimed (Rom. 4:1, 2). 'Nothing of the kind!' replies Paul. Abraham was justified by faith even before he was circumcised (Rom. 4:3-12). The basic promise made to Abraham was entirely dependent on God's grace (Rom. 4:13-22). Exactly the same applies to the Christian believer today (Rom. 4:23-25).

In Galatians Paul takes the argument further. The covenant of grace made with Abraham is the primary source of all understanding of God's dealings with humanity (Gal. 3:7-9). The covenant at Sinai did not follow for another four hundred and thirty years (Gal. 3:15-18). It did not contradict what God had already said. Rather, it drove people to experience the utter futility of trying to earn his favour and approval and thus prepared them to receive what he freely offers (Gal. 3:19-22). It was a kind of parenthesis in God's dealings with people, suited to them in their spiritual infancy until they were ready to enter into the full benefit of his grace; 'our custodian until Christ came, that we might be justified by faith' (Gal. 3:24).

The writer to the Hebrews makes the same point: the 'old covenant' is not by any means the original or the fundamental covenant. Rather it provided a symbol of the real thing, a shadowy foretaste of the full blessing which God wishes to grant (Heb. 10:1). Both before it began and while it lasted, faith was the essential basis of human relationship with God. Throughout the time of the 'old covenant', from Abel to Abraham, from Moses to David, from Samuel to the writing prophets, examples abound of men and women who were 'well attested by their faith' (Heb. 11).

(ii) Children and the covenant

This approach to the one covenant of grace is common to all Reformed theologians. Those who favour paedobaptism take the argument a stage further. They point to an important principle which they find displayed whenever God makes a covenant with men or women: God includes their children in the blessings of the covenant.

In his generation, Noah alone found favour in the eyes of the Lord (Gen. 6:8). Yet God not only saved him from destruction, but his children and their wives as well. Why? Because this is how God deals with those with whom he makes covenants: 'I will establish my covenant with thee [singular]; and thou shalt come into the ark, thou and thy sons, and thy wife, and thy sons' wives with thee' (Gen. 6:18, RV). And again, 'the LORD said unto Noah, Come thou and all thy house into the ark; for thee [singular] have I seen righteous before me in this generation' (Gen. 7:1, RV). Thus Noah's wife, Noah's three sons and their wives were spared the Flood, not because they were righteous but because Noah was righteous.

After the Flood God promised never to destroy the world again.

> Then God said to Noah and to his sons with him, 'Behold, I establish my covenant with you and your descendants after you ... that never again shall all flesh be cut off by the waters of a flood ... This is the sign of the covenant which I make between me and you and every living creature that is with you, for all future generations: I set my bow in the cloud...' (Gen. 9:8-13).

The implications are clear. To this day the human race has survived destruction by deluge, not because it deserves or has earned survival, but because of God's promise to Noah.

God's inclusion of children within his covenant promises is clearly seen in his dealings with Abraham. 'I will establish my covenant between me and you and your descendants after you throughout their generations for an everlasting covenant, to be God to you and to your descendants after you' (Gen. 17:7). Indeed the principle is clear throughout the Old Testament. On one occasion Moses told the Israelites, 'The LORD our God made a covenant with us in Horeb. Not with our fathers did the LORD make this covenant, but with us, who are all of us here alive this day' (Deut. 5:2-3). These Israelites were the children of those to whom God had appeared, for their fathers had died during the forty years' wanderings in the desert. On another occasion, Moses declared, 'the things that are revealed belong to us and to our children for ever' (Deut. 29:29). The psalmist declared that 'the steadfast love of the LORD is from everlasting to everlasting, upon those who fear him, and his righteousness to children's children, to those who keep his covenant and remember to do his commandments' (Ps. 103:17, 18). Isaiah said, 'Fear not, O Jacob my servant ... I will pour my Spirit upon your descendants, and my blessing on your offspring' (Isa. 44:2, 3ff.). And again, of the Messiah he said, 'And he will come to Zion as Redeemer, to those in Jacob who turn from transgression, says the LORD. And as for me, this is my covenant with them, says the LORD: my spirit which is upon you, and my words which I have put in your mouth, shall not depart out of your mouth, or out of the mouth of your children, or out of the mouth of your children's children, says the LORD, from this time forth and for evermore' (Isa. 59:20-21).

Indeed, we cannot understand God's dealings with Israel unless we understand the place of descendants in the covenant. God deals graciously with a wayward and rebellious people throughout the Old Testament because of his covenant with Abraham and his descendants. God requires his people to obey him on the basis of a continuing covenant: 'the things that are revealed belong to us and to our children for ever, that we may do all the words of this law' (Deut. 29:29). Because the Israelites are God's covenant people the prophets plead so strongly with them to turn from their wickedness to their God. Because children are within this covenant they can be and are to be instructed in its terms and conditions (see, for example, Exod. 12:26, 27; 13:8, 14, 15; Deut. 6:20-25).

In the New Testament, God similarly includes children in his covenant with their parents. On the Day of Pentecost Peter declared, 'The promise is to you and to your children' (Acts 2:39). The angel who appeared to Cornelius promised a message by which he would be saved and all his household (Acts 11:14). Paul announced to the Philippian gaoler, 'Believe in the Lord Jesus, and you will be saved, you and your household' (Acts 16:31). Christian wives with unbelieving husbands were comforted with the certainty that their children were holy (1 Cor. 7:14). Children in the churches at Ephesus and Colossae were addressed in the same breath as their parents (Eph. 6:1-3; Col. 3:20).

Thus, the covenant of grace is one, the same in both Old and New Testaments, a covenant of salvation by faith, and also a covenant in which children share its blessings on account of their parents' faith. In the Old Testament the covenant looks forward to Christ, who is clearly foreshadowed, while in the New it looks back to him, but it is still one covenant.

(iii) Signs of the covenant

In the ancient world, human covenant-promises were usually sealed with some kind of ceremony involving both words and signs. God's covenants are similar in this respect. In both Testaments there are words and symbolic signs which accompany the respective covenants.

Although the signs differ, they correspond to each other, and together with the words, speak of Christ. The Old Testament sign of initiation is circumcision. Its matching equivalent in the New is baptism. Circumcision displays Christ, for Paul says, 'In him also [that is, Christ] you were circumcised with a circumcision made without hands, by putting off the body of the flesh in the circumcision of Christ' (Col. 2:11). Baptism corresponds to circumcision, for Paul goes on to say, 'and you were buried with him in baptism, in which you were also raised with him through faith in the working of God, who raised him from the dead' (Col. 2:12).

Similarly, the Old Testament sign of Passover finds its New Testament equivalent in communion. Passover speaks of Christ, for Paul writes, 'Christ, our paschal lamb, has been sacrificed' (1 Cor. 5:7). Communion corresponds to Passover, for it is a sacrament of the new covenant in Christ's blood (see 1 Cor. 11:25). The clear implication is that the church in the New Testament corresponds to Israel in the Old (Gal. 6:16).

Now, who was to be circumcised in Old Testament times? Two types of people: adult converts to the faith of Israel ('proselytes') and the male children of Israelite parents. For both types, circumcision marked their entry into the people of God. To fail to be circumcised was to break God's covenant (Gen. 17:14). So baptism should now be administered to similar groups of people: adult converts to Christianity and the children of Christians. To fail to baptize either is to break God's covenant.

So the argument from covenant theology is complete. Its advocates appeal both to the unity of Scripture and the analogy of Scripture. This, they claim, explains why there is no specific reference in the New Testament to the baptism of infants and little children. Jewish converts to Christianity would automatically have had their children baptized along with themselves. They would have needed a specific command to refrain from so doing; and such a ban cannot be found in the New Testament.

Covenant theologians deny any need for specific New Testament examples of paedobaptism to support their position. They point to another negative: the New Testament never describes the baptism of an adult born of Christian parents! Such a baptism would indeed demonstrate a change in the conditions of entry into the covenant of grace, between the Old and New Testaments. But, they assert, the conditions of entry were not in fact changed. For them, the one covenant of grace and the correspondence between circumcision and baptism gives ample reason for Christian parents to have their children baptized.

(iv) Consequences of covenant theology for paedobaptism

This line of reasoning leads to several important consequences. First, children (and therefore adults) may be members of the visible Christian church without conscious faith. Whatever the place of faith in paedobaptism, children cannot consciously believe, yet in baptism they are admitted into the church. As they grow older they may still not believe, yet, because they are baptized they are members of the church. This raises deeper issues about the nature of the church. We find that we have to keep returning to this.

Many Christians, of course, find no problem with unbelieving people belonging to the church. Indeed, they would accuse baptists of being unrealistic when they attempt to identify the visible church with those who believe. There may indeed be 'nominal', non-practising Christians among those baptized in childhood. But so there are among those baptized as adults too, as an analysis of members in any baptist church would show!

Not only is it unrealistic to demand faith before baptism, it is also unscriptural, so the argument goes. Jesus warned us not to 'judge' (Matt. 7:1); does not an insistence on a church for true Christians only do just that? Paul records of the Jews, God's covenant people, that they 'all were baptized into Moses in the cloud and in the sea ... Nevertheless with most of them God was not pleased; for they were overthrown in the wilderness' (1 Cor. 10:2, 5). Between the Red Sea and the wilderness these Israelites were counted as members of the covenant people and received many of God's blessings to his people. Only later did their true position become apparent when God judged them. Indeed, this is one of Paul's recurring themes, robustly applied to Christians in his generation (Rom. 2:28-29; 9:6-7, 32; and 11:2). As it was with the nation of Israel so it is with the visible church. Many are called, but few are chosen. Only God knows those who are his and he will vindicate them at the last day.

A second consequence of covenant theology for paedobaptism is that baptized children must be regarded as Christians until they give clear evidence to the contrary by their lives. Just because children have been baptized does not mean that they will always be Christians.

As they grow up and learn the implications of the covenant to which they have been admitted, they may decide to reject its terms and conditions and cut themselves off from God's people. They are free to do this. The Israelites were always doing it; hence God's rejection of them as a people (see Rom. 11:7-10). New Testament warnings against apostasy, particularly in the Letter to the Hebrews (see 2:1-3; 4:1-2; 6:4-6; 10:26-29; 12:25), might well have been written to warn Christians baptized in infancy against a similar fate.

Apostasy apart, however, the covenant of grace gives to Christian parents the comfort and assurance that their children belong to God, that he loves them and cares for them and wills to bring them to salvation. The parents, for their part, must observe the terms and conditions of the covenant, particularly as these apply to children. They should train up their children in the way they should go, in the discipline and instruction of the Lord, that when they are old they will not depart from it (see Prov. 22:6; Eph. 6:4). Some indeed will depart from the way, but the majority will not, and while they are children, and until as adults they give clear evidence to the contrary, Christian parents can rest in the confidence that their children belong to Christ and are made regenerate by him.

There is a third implication. To be consistent, covenant theology requires different ways of proclaiming God's Word to those baptized in infancy and those who were not. Everyone breaks God's covenant from time to time and needs to repent and return to him. But those baptized in infancy need to repent, not in order to join God's covenant people, but because they already belong.

After the Bathsheba affair, David pleaded with God for pardon 'according to thy steadfast love; according to thy abundant mercy' (Ps. 51:1). He prayed because he was already a child of the covenant; he asked God to deal with him on its terms. When Peter preached on the Day of Pentecost he offered his audience repentance, baptism and the gift of the Holy Spirit because they were Israelites and already belonged to God's covenant people. When Paul preached at Lystra and at Athens (Acts 15:15-17; 17:22-31), he preached quite differently, commanding his audiences to repent from their idolatry that they might be included in the covenant.

All this, of course, raises intriguing questions about the unity of the gospel. Is there one gospel for the children of Christian parents and another for the rest? Do Christian parents need to look for conversion in their children? At what point, in their growth to adult maturity, do 'Christian' children cross that frightening line into conscious unbelief and thereby reject the blessings of the covenant conferred in their baptism?

Fourthly, paedobaptism in the context of covenant theology has implications for the way baptism is practised. After all, the baptism of children is being based, not on God's universal love, nor on the fact that Jesus blessed babies. It is not even based on the certainty that grace always precedes faith. Quite bluntly, certain children are baptized because they have certain parents. Some kind of 'judging' is required after all! In practice, deciding which children's parents are truly Christian may be more difficult than deciding who should receive baptism because they themselves are truly Christian!

In summary; scriptural support for covenant theology, with its consequences for paedobaptism, is strong. Whatever its difficulties it deserves careful consideration.

e. Baptism and faith

In chapter 1 we referred to the close connection in the New Testament between baptism and faith. Often the two terms are used synonymously. But if faith is so necessary for baptism to be effective, how can a helpless infant believe? Paedobaptists have given three main answers.

Some suggest that in baptism faith is somehow infused into the life of the infant. Before John the Baptist was born Mary, already expecting Jesus, went to visit his mother Elizabeth. 'She entered the house... and greeted Elizabeth. And when Elizabeth heard the greeting of Mary, the babe leaped in her womb... and she exclaimed with a loud cry, " ...when the voice of your greeting came to my ears, the babe in my womb leaped for joy"' (Luke 1:40-44). Moreover, that same child was 'filled with the Holy Spirit, even from his mother's womb' (Luke 1:15). Martin Luther used these passages to claim that an unborn child can believe. Therefore, he concluded, an infant can similarly believe when he or she is baptized. Curiously, it is an idea that has clung to Roman Catholic thinking until this century, but few today, either Roman Catholic or Protestant, find the idea anything but extraordinary. But we may at least recognize that faith can begin long before it can be seen.

A second suggestion is that the church baptizes children in anticipation of their coming faith. Faith indeed is necessary for baptism to be effective, but Scripture nowhere suggests that faith must always precede baptism. It may well follow later and, when it does, it will make the baptism just as effective as when it actually accompanies the rite.

A third proposed answer is that in infant baptism faith is exercised by others on behalf of the child. When parents baptize their children they believe that God loves them, that they are included in his covenant and that he will ultimately bring them to salvation through Christ. The infants may not consciously believe; that does not matter. The parents believe for them. In time, their faith becomes effective. If parents do not believe themselves, if they have died or have abandoned their children, then faith may be exercised by sponsors instead. Along with, or in the absence of, the parents they make the promises and undertake to keep the terms of the covenant. They provide godly upbringing and discipline, so that the children might later believe.

Along with parents and sponsors the church also exercises faith when infants are baptized. The children are admitted into the church. The congregation welcomes them, promises to pray for them and to support their parents in bringing them up. In this way the church believes that, one day, the children will be active in its ranks.

All these ideas, of course, beg the question, can someone believe for someone else, or is it only one's own faith which saves? Naturally, paedobaptists agree we can believe for others. They instance the centurion's servant (Matt. 8:5-13), the paralytic borne by four friends (Matt. 9:1-2), Jairus' daughter (Matt. 9:18, 23-26) and the epileptic boy at the foot of the mount of transfiguration (Matt. 17:14-21) as examples of children and adults healed or raised from the dead when others believed. As might be expected, baptists are not nearly so sure. The point is important, as much of the case for paedobaptism hinges on the answer to the question.

Christians have been baptizing children and infants for at least the last seventeen hundred years, if not from the birth of the church itself. Their reasons have been many and varied. As Calvin said, 'If we would not maliciously obscure the kindness of God, let us present to him our infants, to whom he has assigned a place among his friends and family, that is, the members of the Church.'[10]

References

1. Origen, *Commentary on Romans*, V. ix. 3.
2. Joachim Jeremias, *Infant Baptism in the First Four Centuries* (English translation: SCM, 1960), p. 66
3. *Letter of the church of Smyrna*, IX. 3. Quoted in J. Stevenson, *A New Eusebius* (SPCK, 1960), p. 21.
4. See e.g. Dom Gregory Dix, *The Theology of Confirmation in Relation to Baptism* (Dacre Press, 1946), p. 31, footnote 2.
5. Justin, *First Apology*, 15.6.
6. See above p. 17.
7. *The Alternative Service Book, 1980*, p. 246.
8. Church of Scotland interim report of commission on baptism, 1955, p. 10.
9. *The Biblical Doctrine of Baptism* (study document issued by Special Commission of the Church of Scotland, 1958), p. 42.
10. John Calvin, *Institutes*, IV. xviii. 32.

3

The Baptist Approach

Paedobaptists, as we have seen, justify their position in many different ways. In contrast, the baptist approach is disarmingly simple. Every doctrinal statement about baptism in the New Testament presupposes conscious faith in Christ in those who are baptized. Every instance of baptism recorded in the New Testament is of men or women who wish to express their faith in Christ. Philip's reply to the Ethiopian eunuch's question, 'What is to prevent my being baptized?' is paramount: 'If you believe with all your heart, you may' (see Acts 8:36 and footnote to verse 37).[1]

For baptists, these words reflect the universal yardstick of the apostolic church in administering baptism: conscious faith on the part of the candidate. When faith was present, baptism could proceed. If faith was absent, baptism must wait. As the famous Victorian preacher C. H. Spurgeon said, 'I consider that the "baptism" of an unconscious infant is just as foolish as the "baptism" of a ship or a bell, for there is as much Scripture for the one as for the other.'[2] Consequently, baptists are left unimpressed by the evidence for paedobaptism offered in the previous chapter.

Historical evidence

Accounts of family and household baptisms in the New Testament are dismissed. Either there were no infants in the families concerned, or infants were specifically excluded because they were infants. If infants were baptized in Cornelius' household, the story requires us to believe that they also spoke in tongues and extolled God! (See Acts 10:46-48.) If any children were baptized in the Philippian gaoler's family they must have been old enough to believe, for that is what Paul and Silas told them to do! (See Acts 16:33.) If infants were included in household baptisms in Corinth (1 Cor. 1:16), they must have been precocious indeed, for we later learn that 'the household of Stephanas ... devoted themselves to the service of the saints' (1 Cor. 16:15). If infants were included in the baptism they must have shared in the subsequent service!

To the baptist, New Testament household baptisms do not illustrate family solidarity, but merely record that on several occasions whole families responded to the gospel. Thus, at Caesarea, 'the Holy Spirit fell on all who heard the word' (Acts 10:44). In Philippi, Paul and Silas baptized all to whom they had previously spoken the word of the Lord (see Acts 16:32). At Corinth, 'Crispus, the ruler of the synagogue, believed in the Lord, together with all his household' (Acts 18:8). New Testament family baptisms would appear to deny rather than exemplify paedobaptism.

Indeed, many baptists are dubious about the whole idea of family solidarity as it is popularly expressed. After all, Jesus warned that his gospel can divide families as readily as it unites them:

> Do not think that I have come to bring peace on earth; I have not come to bring peace, but a sword. For I have come to set a man against his father, and a daughter against her mother, and a daughter-in-law against her mother-in-law; and a man's foes will be those of his own household (Matt. 10:34-36).

Paul's and Peter's letters deal with the practical problems of families that are *not* united in faith (see 1 Cor. 7:14; 1 Pet. 3:1-6). In itself the principle of family solidarity provides no justification for paedobaptism.

Nor are baptists too impressed with evidence from the Fathers. Origen's statement about the apostolic origin of paedobaptism is very dubious when balanced against Tertullian's clearly expressed doubts.[3] The argument from Polycarp's martyrdom founders on our ignorance of his age when he died. His own words contain no explicit reference to baptism, only to serving Christ from an early age. Baptists do not deny that children can believe, nor, strictly speaking, do they deny baptism to believing children.

As for Jewish proselyte baptism, there is no evidence to prove that it influenced Christian baptism, and there are scholarly doubts as to whether it existed as early as the first half of the first century.[4] In this connection Paul's assertion that the children of a half-Christian family are 'holy' (1 Cor. 7:14) proves too much if it is used to support paedobaptism, for Paul also asserts that the unbelieving partner is similarly 'consecrated'. If the 'holy' children should be baptized, so should the 'consecrated' partners, yet this is nonsense, for in the next breath Paul insists that these partners are 'unbelieving' and need to be saved (see 1 Cor. 7:15-16).

The complete silence of the New Testament concerning paedo-baptism settles the issue for baptists. Baptism should be given only to those who consciously believe in Christ and are determined to live for him.

Theological evidence
When baptists look behind New Testament baptismal narratives to their theological significance, they reject paedobaptism more firmly than ever. They are unimpressed by the arguments outlined in the previous chapter. They also find in Scripture a positive theology of the church, of salvation and of baptism which forbids them to baptize infants and requires them to baptize conscious believers only.

a. The purpose of baptism
Along with the majority of Protestants, most baptists have accepted (with various modifications) Augustine's doctrine of original sin. They believe that we are all flawed at the heart of our humanity, and that somehow we have inherited this condition from our parents. But they do not regard baptism as the solution to this problem. Christ's work on the cross redeems us from the curse of sin. His redemption is received by faith. There is no other way. Unbaptized children who die before they are old enough to commit conscious sin will be received into heaven by a loving Father where they will learn of Christ and grow in him. To make baptism itself, without conscious faith, a condition of entry into heaven is to give it a significance and importance which baptists cannot find in the New Testament. Baptism, as they see it, is essentially a declaration of people to God, not a declaration of God to people.

b. Jesus and children
For baptists, the Gospel accounts of Jesus receiving and blessing children (Matt. 18:3; 19:13-15; Mark 10:13-16; Luke 18:15-17) are irrelevant to the baptismal debate. First, the passages say nothing about baptism, nothing at all. They record an incident in the life of Jesus when he welcomed children, blessed them and said some important things about receiving the kingdom of God. But as Jesus made no reference to baptism, no conclusions about the rite can be deduced.

Secondly, with the exception of Luke 18:15, the passages describe how children, not infants, were brought to Jesus, so even if they were relevant to baptism they would only justify child baptism, not infant baptism. In this connection care must be taken not to make too much of Luke's reference. Two out of three say children were brought to Jesus and all three agree that Jesus said, 'Let the children come to me' (see particularly Luke 18:16). Even if infants were among those brought to Jesus, most were children old enough to come or turn away.

Thirdly, to justify paedobaptism from the passages in question would make nonsense of Jesus' related remarks about receiving the kingdom. Jesus was speaking to his disciples, to adults. He was telling them how to receive the kingdom. Receiving the kingdom is a conscious thing: 'whoever does not receive the kingdom of God like a child shall not enter it'; 'unless you turn and become like children, you will never enter the kingdom of heaven'. Infants can never set an example to adults here, for infants cannot make conscious choices.

Finally, entering the kingdom of God involves humility and trust: 'whoever humbles himself like this child, he is the greatest in the kingdom of heaven'. Children find this easier than adults because of their childlike character, but they must still receive the kingdom as infants cannot do. Nothing in all this contradicts baptist theology, indeed it supports it. Entry into the kingdom comes through conscious humble faith. Baptism is the sacred visible sign of faith and therefore should be received only by those who consciously believe.

c. Baptism and salvation

Most baptists agree that God is the author of salvation and that his grace works in our lives long before we consciously believe in him. But to baptize infants to witness to God's prevenient grace is, baptists suggest, to distort the purpose of baptism. If this is the case, then all infants should be baptized, for no-one can know in whom God's grace will issue in faith and salvation. Yet, when infants are baptized indiscriminately the result is millions of baptized pagans, as in Western Europe at the present time. Many paedobaptists themselves are increasingly uneasy with this situation.

That God's prevenient grace is taught in Scripture is indisputable. But baptism does not witness to this truth. Baptism symbolizes the equally important truth that grace demands and prompts the response of faith. Faith, for the baptist, is paramount. Baptism without conscious faith is not New Testament baptism and is therefore invalid.

d. Baptism and the covenant of grace
Baptists respond variously to paedobaptist arguments in this area.

(i) Baptists who reject covenant theology
Many baptists reject the idea that Scripture reveals one covenant in Old and New Testament alike. They see discontinuity and contrast between the two parts of the Bible. For example, Jeremiah promises a 'new covenant... not like the covenant which I made with their fathers' (Jer. 31:31, 32). At the Last Supper Jesus said, 'This cup is the new covenant in my blood' (1 Cor. 11:25). Paul, writing to the Galatians, makes a great deal of the two covenants (Gal. 4:24), and the author of the Letter to the Hebrews builds a whole argument on the ministry of Christ 'as much more excellent than the old as the covenant he mediates is better, since it is enacted on better promises ... Therefore he is the mediator of a new covenant' (see Heb. 8–10, particularly 8:6 and 9:15). An imperfect and incomplete covenant lies at the heart of the Old Testament; 'our custodian until Christ came' (Gal. 3:24).

In the new covenant, baptists insist, the position of children is radically altered. Peter's pentecostal promise, 'to you and to your children', is qualified with the words, 'every one whom the Lord our God calls to him' (Acts 2:39). The 'call' involves repentance and baptism, in that order. Children no longer enter into relationship with God through natural birth into one select nation; God's grace is now offered to people of all nations through penitent faith. Many who believe will of course be children. They are addressed in Paul's letters (e.g. Eph. 6:1-3), not because they are the children of Christians, but because they are Christian believers themselves. Paul also assumes there will be sad examples of Christians' children who will not believe. How else can he insist that elders, for example, should have believing families? (see Titus 1:6).

Any other position contradicts the whole trend of New Testament teaching. If Christians' children are born within the covenant of grace, how could Jesus say that 'that which is born of the flesh is flesh' (John 3:6), and 'unless one is born anew, he cannot see the kingdom of God' (John 3:3)? How could John, commenting on these words, underline the stark distinction between being born of God and being born of human parents (see John 1:12-13)? If a person is baptized in infancy, how can he in later life fail to be other than confused about his need for a personal encounter with God?

Baptists who reject covenant theology naturally reject arguments for paedobaptism based on parallels with circumcision. Of course circumcision marked entry into the old covenant just as baptism marks entry into the new, but this does not mean they should be administered in the same way. Indeed, the reverse is the case. Circumcision and baptism are linked in the New Testament only in Colossians 2:11-14. These verses cannot be used to justify paedobaptism in view of clear warnings elsewhere. Paul asserts, for example, that true circumcision is not something external and physical, but is a matter of the heart; spiritual and not literal (see Rom. 2:28-29). In other words, the Christian receives true circumcision through encounter with the crucified Saviour. Baptism singles out and underlines this. Burial and resurrection with Christ come 'through faith in the working of God, who raised him from the dead' (Col. 2:12). Infants and little children cannot believe like this and so should not be baptized.

Paul's treatment of circumcision in his letter to the Galatians is even more emphatic. There he is fiercely combating the insistence of some Jewish Christians that Gentile converts should be circumcised. His reply is not simply that baptism has now replaced circumcision (how had the argument ever arisen if that was the simple equation?), but that faith responding to God's grace (expressed in baptism) has replaced commitment to legalistic effort (expressed in circumcision). If circumcision as a ceremony had the importance which covenant theologians give it, could Paul have written such words? And did the apostle, demolishing false reliance on a ceremony thought to have saving power to whole families, proceed to replace it with another ceremony thought to do exactly the same? Clearly not! Circumcision and baptism are as different from each other as the covenants into which they mark entrance. Because they are so different, infant circumcision cannot be used to justify infant baptism.

(ii) Baptists who accept covenant theology

Most denominational Baptists reject paedobaptism because they reject the idea of a single covenant of grace. However, many baptists stand within a strongly Calvinistic tradition and accept covenant theology. Yet they still refuse to baptize infants. They do not quarrel with the premise (one covenant of grace, accepted by faith, in Old and New Testaments), but with the conclusion (the automatic inclusion of all believers' children in that covenant). They argue bluntly that paedobaptists make a double mistake. They practise something for which there is no specific command in the New Testament, and they commit themselves to a theory which is contradicted by specific New Testament statements, and even Old Testament teaching.[5]

The original covenant made with Abraham included two distinct elements, one physical and the other spiritual. For example, it promised a literal portion of land: 'I will give this land' (Gen. 12:7); yet it gave a foretaste of a spiritual inheritance: 'he looked forward to the city which has foundations, whose builder and maker is God', and 'they desire a better country, that is, a heavenly one' (Heb. 11:10, 16). As David Kingdon puts it, the covenant had both dispensational and transdispensational elements, the first fulfilled before Christ's coming, the second as a result of his coming.[6]

Thus, the word 'seed' or 'descendants' had a double meaning. Abraham's physical descendants would possess the land of Canaan (Gen. 12:7), but his spiritual descendants would be all those with a faith like his (see Rom. 4:16). Similarly, circumcision had two purposes: to mark out a special nationality ('the circumcised') and to symbolize moral and spiritual characteristics seen only in some (as Moses and the prophets never tired of saying).

Circumcision was the sacrament of a national group who were given a physical country, inherited by their natural offspring. For this reason it was taken up into the national system given at Sinai. But it also symbolized the change of heart granted to people with faith. Therefore it was used in the covenant of grace, a covenant central to, yet also foretold in, the Old Testament, and brought to fruition in the New. In the New Testament, this covenant finds its fulfilment in the reality of new birth. The Christian equivalent of circumcision, therefore, is not baptism but regeneration. As Paul says, 'we are the true circumcision, who worship God in spirit, and glory in Christ Jesus' (Phil. 3:3), and 'real circumcision is a matter of the heart, spiritual and not literal' (Rom. 2:29).

What then of the promise made to 'your descendants' (Gen. 17:7)? This applied only to the natural descendants of Abraham during the dispensational period of the covenant. Transdispensationally, Abraham's descendants are those who display his faith. The promise is not that the children of Jews or the children of Christians are automatically included in the covenant, but that there will always be a believing company. It is as simple as that. There is nothing here of two ways of salvation, one by new birth, and the other via birth into a godly family. The New Testament references to families are simply particular applications of the universal message that whoever believes shall live. And, of course, whoever believes should be baptized; the symbol then (and only then) corresponds to the reality.

Baptists who accept covenant theology deny that it leads to infant baptism. They join with baptists who reject covenant theology in opposing paedobaptist conclusions (as outlined above). Indeed, all baptists insist that their position is much more positive than a simple denial of paedobaptist arguments. They assert that biblical teaching about the church, the gospel and the doctrine of baptism all support their position.

e. The doctrine of the church
Baptists often maintain that, in spite of their name, their distinctive position is not that of baptism, but of a specific view of the church. They insist that the New Testament knows only a church made up of professing believers. They find that faith is mentioned whenever entry into the church is described.

Thus, on the Day of Pentecost, those who received Peter's word were baptized (Acts 2:41). After the healing of the man who sat at the Beautiful Gate of the Temple, 'many of those who heard the word believed' (Acts 4:4). After the burial of Ananias and Sapphira and following the signs and wonders done by the hands of the apostles 'more than ever believers were added to the Lord' (Acts 5:14). After the appointment of the seven deacons 'the word of God increased; and the number of disciples multiplied greatly in Jerusalem, and a great many of the priests were obedient to the faith' (Acts 6:7). When the Samaritans believed Philip as he preached good news about the kingdom of God and the name of Jesus Christ, they were baptized, both men and women (Acts 8:12). This, say baptists, is the unchanging pattern. New Testament churches are composed of 'saints who are also faithful in Christ Jesus' (Eph. 1:1). This is the test which must be applied when baptism is requested: 'If you believe with all your heart, you may' (Acts 8:37, footnote).

A corollary of the baptist position is the concept of the 'gathered church'. Although this is shared by some paedobaptists, it is fundamentally a baptist position. The church cannot be equated with a nation, for the people of a nation are too diverse to be all 'faithful brethren in Christ' (Col. 1:2). Nor can one belong to the church by virtue of one's place of birth, for that would deprive faith of its primary place in the economy of salvation.

This is the broader ground on which baptists base their position. For them the Christian church is made up of Christians. 'Baptism for Baptists is a matter of churchmanship,' argued one of their best-known apologists. 'Because they have a high and holy conception of its membership, they feel that baptism should only be administered to those who understand its true significance and personally accept its solemn responsibilities.'[7]

Writing to the bishops of the Church of England in 1926 Baptists maintained,

> We believe in the Catholic Church as the holy society of believers in our Lord Jesus Christ ... We believe this holy society is truly to be found wherever companies of believers united as churches on the ground of a confession of personal faith ... Because we hold the Church to be a community of Christian believers, the ordinance of Baptism is administered among us to those only who make a personal confession of repentance and faith.[8]

This is the positive basis of the practice of baptism for adults only. Whether or not it is convincing to other Christians, it deserves to be understood and respected. Baptists are not nasty sectarians who deny that God loves little children, but high church men and women who do not wish to confuse the church with the world or with the nation, or with Israel.

Baptism stands at the door of the church; a church that opens to receive believers and closes to exclude unbelievers. Once a Christian community begins to welcome the unbeliever, the half-believer and the infant incapable of belief within its actual membership, that community will begin to lose its spiritual zeal and its evangelical experience.

f. The doctrine of salvation
Throughout the New Testament faith is the key to salvation. Justification by faith is the article of a standing or falling church, as Martin Luther declared. But the unregenerate human heart rebels against complete dependence upon God and longs to boast of earning its own favour with him. The gospel of the grace of God is constantly

threatened and corrupted by additions which give sinful people the privilege of doing something for themselves instead of stretching out empty hands to God. Christians must always guard against suggestions that their salvation partly depends on their decency, their performance of religious efforts or their progress in personal morality. The New Testament warns against this danger, and Christian history traces its constant recurrence. 'By grace you have been saved through faith' (Eph. 2:8) is the consistent message of the Bible. In the Bible, when baptism is linked with faith, it is clearly as an expression of faith and of faith alone.

Now the baptist believes that the only way to protect baptism itself from becoming a snare and a false means of salvation itself is to insist that the connection between baptism and faith is clear, recognizable, fundamental and unequivocal. He fears that this is not so in the case of an infant. To identify the faith involved with the parents, the sponsors, the church or the hope that one day the infant will believe, is not sufficient. It puts a gap in time or condition between the act of baptism and the personal faith of the candidate. In this way it focuses attention in the wrong place. The blessings associated in Scripture with faith-plus-baptism will, in paedobaptism, unavoidably be associated with the baptism rather than the faith. However much is said about faith coming later, the process has started off on the wrong foot. Many people baptized in infancy will grow up unaware of the need to come in personal faith. The only safeguard is to keep baptism until faith is expressed.

g. The doctrine of baptism
If faith is the key to salvation, what is the place and meaning of baptism? To answer this question baptists insist that we must go beyond asking how the apostles practised baptism, and ask how they explained it. Throughout the New Testament forgiveness of sins, new birth, the gift of the Holy Spirit, identification with Christ in his death and resurrection, are all associated with faith, and with faith-expressed-in-baptism.

Infants cannot exercise faith. This blunt fact makes the baptism of infants so fundamentally different from the baptism of believing adults that baptists feel compelled to regard it as a different rite altogether. In contrast to it, believers' baptism makes different requirements of the candidate, is differently related to the preaching of the gospel, and is differently connected to the blessings associated with baptism. The New Testament describes and explains believers' baptism; it does neither for infant baptism. Therefore most baptists do not feel able to give the name baptism to a ceremony to which small children are brought. This is not a matter of bigotry, but of deep theological moment. Baptists deserve understanding, if not agreement.

As C. H. Spurgeon, the prince of English Victorian preachers put it:

> If we could find (infant baptism) in the Word of God, we should adopt it. It would help us out of a great difficulty, for it would take away from us that reproach which is attached to us – that we are odd and do not as other people do. But we have looked well through the Bible and cannot find it, and do not believe it is there; nor do we believe that others can find infant baptism in the Scriptures, unless they themselves first put it there.[9]

References

1. We recognize that the earliest manuscripts of the Acts of the Apostles do not contain Philip's reply to the Ethiopian eunuch's question, but the account still points the way even without the footnote; it is a story of dawning and declared faith. Philip's reply is also held to reflect the understanding of the early church on this vital question.
2. C. H. Spurgeon, *The Early Years* (Banner of Truth, 1967), p. 149.
3. See chapter 4.
4. See George Beasley-Murray, *Baptism in the New Testament* (Macmillian, 1963), pp. 18-30.
5. The two main English exponents of this view in the 1970s were Paul King Jewett in *Infant Baptism and Confirmation* (unpublished), and David Kingdon in *Children of Abraham* (Henry B. Walter, 1973).
6. David Kingdon, *op. cit.*, p 29.
7. Henry Cook, *What Baptists Stand For* (Carey Kingsgate Press, 1947), p. 89.
8. The reply of the Baptist Union to the Lambeth Appeal.
9. Spurgeon, *op. cit.* pp. 154-155.

Part 2

Baptism and History

4

After the Apostles

Tertullian

During the closing decade of the second century a brilliant young barrister was converted to Christ in the bustling North African city of Carthage. Of the circumstances surrounding his conversion we know little, but we do know that remarkably soon afterwards Quintus Septimius Florens Tertullianus (known to history as Tertullian) became one of the most outstanding Christians of his day and left in his writings a legacy which has influenced the church ever since. Because Tertullian was the first major Christian thinker to write in Latin, his terminology has defined theology in the Western church and its offshoots ever since.

Addressing himself to the needs of the moment, Tertullian wrote fluently on a variety of subjects. First, he vigorously defended the Christian faith against the persecuting attacks of Roman governors. Then he produced theological, ethical and disciplinary treatises for Christians themselves, much in the way the apostle Paul had composed his letters to the members of the infant church. And when 'a certain female viper from the Cainite sect ... carried off a good number with her exceptionally pestilential doctrine, making a particular point of demolishing baptism',[1] Tertullian addressed himself to the subject and produced *de Baptismo*, his *Homily on baptism.*

de baptismo is supremely important for modern baptismal issues because it contains the first explicit reference in all Christian writing, Scripture included, to paedobaptism; significantly, it protests against it. Tertullian writes:

> It follows that deferment of baptism is more profitable, in accordance with each person's character and attitude, and even age: and especially so as regards children. For what need is there, if there really is no need, for even their sponsors to be brought into peril, seeing they may possibly themselves fail of their promises by death, or be deceived by the subsequent development of an evil disposition? It is true our Lord says, 'Forbid them not to come to me.' So let them come, when they are growing up, when they are learning, when they are being taught what they are

coming to: let them be made Christians when they have become competent to know Christ. Why should innocent infancy come with haste to the
remission of sins? Shall we take less cautious action in this than we take
in worldly matters? Shall one who is not trusted with earthly property be
entrusted with heavenly? Let them first learn how to ask for salvation, so
that you may be seen to have given to one that asketh. With no less
reason ought the unmarried also to be delayed until they either marry or
are firmly established in continence: until then, temptation lies in wait
for them, for virgins because they are ripe for it, and for widows because
of their wandering about. All who understand what a burden baptism is
will have more fear of obtaining it than of its postponement. Faith unimpaired has no doubt of its salvation.[2]

If some of Tertullian's arguments sound strange to modern ears,
others possess a familiar ring. Concerning infant baptism, however,
against what was Tertullian protesting – an old-established practice
reaching back to the days of the apostles themselves, or a new development taking place throughout the church at the turn of the second
and third centuries? Scholars have debated this question as keenly as
the wider issue itself.[3] Whatever the answer, within thirty years of the
publication of *De Baptismo* Hippolytus in the West and Origen in the
East both regarded infant baptism as normal, deriving its origin and
authority from the apostles. Equally significant is the fact that Tertullian's concerns about paedobaptism were part of a wider protest against
hasty baptism in general, in which virgins and widows were particularly included. All this arose out of the way baptism was understood
in the post-apostolic church.

The *Didache*

Three surviving sources describe the development of early Christian
baptismal belief and practice up to the turn of the second and third
centuries – the time of Tertullian's treatise. The first of these is the
Didache or *Teaching of the Twelve Apostles*. Some scholars date this
between 50 and 110! It constantly echoes Matthew's Gospel, which
was universally regarded as the 'normative' Gospel by the end of the
first century, and frequently used for evangelism and basic Christian
teaching. The *Didache* fulfilled a similar role, but was not regarded
as 'inspired scripture'. In this little book baptism is preceded by fasting and is administered in the threefold Name in running water. If
running water or a pool is not available, water may be poured on the
head three times.[4]

Justin Martyr

Next comes the *First Apology* of Justin Martyr, written about the middle of the second century. Justin came to Christianity because he was dissatisfied with the philosophies of his day. Having been converted, he presented the Roman authorities, in his Apologies, with a reasoned defence of Christianity. Sadly, his efforts were of little avail, for, as his name implies, he died as a martyr in Rome about 163 during the reign of the Emperor Marcus Aurelius.

Baptism, for Justin, is the means whereby men and women are dedicated to God and made new through Christ. It is given to 'as many as are persuaded and believe that the things are true which are taught by the church and undertake to be able to live accordingly'. It is preceded by prayer and fasting by the candidates and congregation. Then they are brought where there is water and are born again, being washed in the Name of the Father, the Son and the Holy Spirit. Baptism is administered that the baptized may obtain remission of sins formerly committed. It is followed by prayers and the celebration of communion along with the assembled congregation.[5]

Hippolytus

The third important source which reflects early Christian baptismal belief and practice is the *Apostolic Tradition* of Hippolytus. Scholars generally consider this to describe the practice of the church in Rome at the turn of the second and third centuries. Here, baptism is much more elaborate than in the earlier accounts. It is preceded by anointing with the oil of exorcism and prayer for the departure of spirits. Threefold baptism by immersion is then accompanied by interrogation and affirmation of belief in the clauses of the Apostles' Creed. Further anointing follows with the oil of thanksgiving, the laying-on of hands by the bishop and prayers. In baptism, remission of sins is obtained through the laver of regeneration of the Holy Spirit.[6]

These early descriptions of baptism reflect the phenomenal growth of the church which was taking place by the end of the second century. Although still officially illegal, Christianity was fast becoming very popular. It frequently came into conflict with the Roman authorities for that very reason. Its growing influence was regarded by successive emperors with suspicion and fear. Its voice was heard throughout Europe and the Near East. Large numbers were pressing into its ranks for a mixture of reasons: its social concern, its superior morality, its kindness to the slave, its words of certainty about the after-life.

Because the church was growing so rapidly, by no means all of its converts had really turned from paganism. Periodic times of persecution thinned out the ranks of the half-converted, but after the official 'recognition' of Christianity by the Emperor Constantine in 313 by the Edict of Milan, the growth rate became an avalanche. In these circumstances it is hardly surprising that the outward trappings of the faith made more appeal than its deeper convictions. And since baptism was the means of entry into the church, it is no less surprising that changes in the administration and understanding of baptism reflected the growing importance and position of Christianity.

Baptismal preparation

Compared with the New Testament itself, accounts of baptism in the early church show three areas of development: the extent of baptismal preparation, the way the rite is administered, and the way the rite is understood.

In the New Testament itself there is little or no preparation for baptism. Thus the Pentecostal converts were baptized on the same day as they heard the gospel (Acts 2:41). The Ethiopian eunuch was baptized when convenient water was reached by the roadside (Acts 8:37). The Philippian gaoler was baptized 'the same hour of the night' as he believed in the Lord Jesus (Acts 16:33). In the post-apostolic church this was all changed. In the *Didache* baptism was administered only when the candidates had 'first recited all these things', that is, all things concerning the Way of Life and the Way of Death, the subject matter of the manual.[7] In Justin, baptism was given only to 'as many as are persuaded and believe that the things are true which are taught by us and said to be true, and undertake to be able to live accordingly'.[8] This implies a period of instruction and probation beforehand. In Hippolytus, assent to the Apostles' Creed during baptism would not have been required without previous instruction in its meaning.

Rapid growth during the church's early centuries made baptismal preparation necessary. By Hippolytus' time the system of preparation had become institutionalized into the 'Catechumenate'. Catechumens were people anxious to join the church but kept in a period of probation until they were considered to be ready for full membership. Regarded as Christians, they were permitted to attend all the services, but not to take communion. For three years they received moral and religious teaching. Then, those who still wished were received into full church membership and were baptized. The rest could remain as catechumens, in the outer circle of church activity. The whole process was thoughtful and impressive. To increase its effectiveness, the act of baptism was invested with a tremendous aura of solemnity and crisis. All of the long catechetical teaching pointed towards it. A theology of baptism gave it immense significance. Every artifice of symbol and ceremony was used to make the baptismal service a memorable occasion.

The catechetical lectures of Cyril, Bishop of Jerusalem in the fourth century, show clearly the development of this practice to a peak of near-perfection. Carefully constructed, they cover every aspect of Christianity. The lessons themselves are punctuated by impressive symbolic acts. Each lesson begins as the bishop breathes on the catechists, covers their heads, exorcises them and reads solemn scriptural warnings.

After detailed instruction on Christian ethics and doctrine, the bishop eventually reaches the baptismal lessons themselves. He warns his hearers that this is a secret which should not be shared with unbelievers. 'We are handing on to you a mystery, a hope of the Age to come. Guard the mystery from those who would waste this prize.'[9] He then refers to the sixth chapter of Romans and expounds its symbolism of death and resurrection with Christ. 'Christ is here in your midst,' he concludes dramatically. 'He is ready, O you who want to be baptized, to bring you by the Holy Spirit into the presence of the Father.'[10]

The baptismal service eventually takes place at dawn on Easter Sunday, in the floor of the sepulchre, believed to be the very site of Christ's tomb. No effort is spared to make the ceremony deeply impressive with its flaming torches, chanting voices, white-robed candidates, solemn questions, ceremonies of exorcism, anointing, laying-on of hands and the threefold immersion of perhaps several hundred converts.

Baptismal practice
Cyril's baptismal service highlights the second important development in early church baptism; the way the rite is administered. In the

New Testament and in the *Didache*, baptism is a simple affair involving little more than immersion or affusion in the Name of Jesus or perhaps of the Trinity. By the time of Hippolytus and Cyril all this has changed. To the actual washing of baptism has been added exorcism, anointing and the episcopal laying-on of hands, quite apart from embellishments surrounding the act itself. When this change is linked with the understanding given to baptism in the fourth century, it is easy to see how the stage was set for medieval developments which would be challenged at the Reformation.

Baptismal understanding
In their understanding of baptism the early Fathers stressed its connection with forgiveness more than anything else. Thus, for example, Justin said that baptism was administered that 'we ... may obtain the remission of sins formerly committed'.[11] Hippolytus affirmed that the baptized were made 'worthy to obtain remission of sins through the laver of regeneration of the Holy Spirit'.[12]

If baptism secured the forgiveness of sins, what of sins committed after baptism? Was there any forgiveness for these? Initially, the answer was, No, although later the appalling implications of this conclusion forced theologians to distinguish between sins for which there was forgiveness (later still called venial sins) and sins for which there was no forgiveness (mortal sins). Tertullian himself followed this line of thinking, listing the 'deadly sins' of idolatry, blasphemy, murder, adultery, fornication, false witness and fraud for which there was no forgiveness if they were committed after baptism.[13]

If post-baptismal sin were unforgivable, might it not be better to delay baptism, even to the point of death, in order to avoid apostasy and to die in the certainty of forgiveness? To many Christians, particularly during the fourth century when thousands were flocking into the church, this was particularly attractive.

While the reasoning is not carried to this conclusion by Tertullian its beginnings are clearly to be found in his thought.

> Deferment of baptism is more profitable, in accordance with each person's character and attitude.... With no less reason ought the unmarried also to be delayed until they either marry or are firmly established in continence: until then, temptation lies in wait for them.... All who understand what a burden baptism is will have more fear of obtaining it than of its postponement.[14]

For the same reason children should not be baptized lest their sponsors be found to have made promises for those in whom 'an evil disposition' subsequently develops.

Original sin

When, early in the third century, Origen described the baptism of little children as a tradition handed down from the apostles[15] he also recognised he had a problem. If baptism was for the forgiveness of sins, from what sin or sins did little children need to be forgiven?[16] Cyprian, Bishop of Carthage in North Africa later in the century, supplied the answer: from the sin of Adam.[17] If sin came into the world through one man and death through sin, and if death spread to everyone because everyone sinned (Rom. 5:12), then even little children needed to be baptized to be forgiven for the sin they had inherited from their parents.

Cyprian's answer was fine as far as it went, but it posed another question: how exactly is Adam's sin inherited by his descendants? Augustine of Hippo (also in North Africa) addressed that question a hundred and fifty years later, at the turn of the fourth and fifth centuries.

Augustine believed that in baptism everyone received, not just the Holy Spirit, but also the seal of the Spirit whereby they were marked as belonging to Christ and able to receive his grace. He also believed, with Cyprian, that everyone was tainted with the sin of Adam. The child not only received the seed of its body from its father but its soul as well. Since the father's soul was sinful – from Adam – so was the child's. As the father needed baptism, so did the child. And was not the church's practice of paedobaptism evidence for the rightness of the church's belief in original sin? The baptism of children confirmed the theology, rather than the other way round!

Augustine's doctrine of original sin became part of orthodox belief in the Roman Catholic and, later, Protestant churches. But what started as an argument from paedobaptism soon became an argument for the baptism of children. Augustine took the argument to its logical conclusion. If baptized children were saved, then unbaptized children were damned, eternally![18] One hears the same fear today, from unbelieving materialistic, hedonistic parents in late twentieth-century Britain who still, from motives buried deeply in folk-religion, seek Christian baptism for their newly born children.

Sign and sacrament

During the early Roman Empire parties to a lawsuit or legal contract would deposit a sum of money or a title deed to property in a religious temple. The one who lost the lawsuit or who broke the contract would then forfeit the money or the property. The money or deed placed in the temple was called a *sacramentum*. Later, the same word was applied to the oath of allegiance made by soldiers to their commander and to the gods of Rome. In each case the *sacramentum* involved a religious ceremony in a sacred place.

By the second century AD Christians were calling baptism a *sacramentum*, for that was what it was. Baptism was the oath of allegiance made by Christians to their Captain, Jesus Christ. In the Church of England's baptismal ceremony today, and in many other ceremonies, the newly baptized are still urged: 'Do not be ashamed to confess the faith of Christ crucified,' and the people reply: 'Fight valiantly under the banner of Christ against sin, the world, and the devil, and continue his faithful soldiers and servants to the end of your lives.'[19]

Once the term *sacramentum* or sacrament was applied to baptism, Christians began to apply it to other ceremonies as well, particularly the eucharist or holy communion. During the fourth and fifth centuries, any sacred symbol or ceremony came to be called a *sacramentum*. Augustine defined a sacrament as 'a sign of a sacred reality'.

In chapter 1 we showed, from the New Testament, how baptism is a sign of repentance, forgiveness, reception of the Holy Spirit, the primacy of God's grace, the Christian's participation in the death and resurrection of Christ, and the Christian's inheritance of eternal life. All of these are received in baptism through faith. Without faith it is impossible to please God (Heb. 11:6). So, if faith is paramount, why baptize? The dying thief was promised a place in Paradise without baptism (Luke 23:43). Why do we need a sign of the sacred reality?

Christians baptize because Jesus told them to (Matt. 28:19). Christians baptize because the apostles baptized and filled their New Testament letters with teaching about its meaning, its significance and its importance. Baptism, for most Christians, is part of the obedience of faith. Baptism and faith are so closely linked that, in a sense, you can't have one without the other!

When baptism began to be described as a sacrament, however, a new dimension was added to the debate. For, from being merely signs of sacred reality, sacraments also began to be described as means of grace. They enjoyed value in themselves, and were to be received accordingly.

If sacraments are means of grace, how does grace flow through them? By the second half of the twelfth century theologians were saying that baptism and the other sacraments bring God's grace to the recipient *ex opere operato*, that is, 'by the work being worked'. So, to put it crudely, if 'baptism saves you', then the act of baptism in itself automatically brings salvation. Nothing else is required. Faith may be desirable but is ultimately unnecessary.

Since the Reformation in the sixteenth century Protestants have often pilloried Roman and other Catholics for such teaching. They have accused them of encouraging belief in the mere act of baptism as the automatic way to heaven. And it has to be said that, at times, some Catholic Christians have encouraged this view. The *conquista-dores* of central and southern America, for example, were not averse to 'baptizing' whole villages with a sort of ecclesiastical stirrup pump which sprayed them with holy water! Nor were they averse to torturing and killing the villagers if they did not behave like good Catholics thereafter!

But in fairness, it is equally true that Catholic theologians from the Middle Ages onwards have never understood *ex opere operato* in such a crudely literal and magical sense. Baptism brings God's grace *non ponentibus obicem*: 'in the case of those who place no impediment.' Lack of faith, particularly in adults, is such an impediment and hinders the reception of grace. The place of faith when infants are baptized is keenly debated, as we have shown. Moreover, the original emphasis on *ex opere operato* was intended to provide a safeguard *against* a mechanical and superstitious understanding of what happens in a sacrament. Suppose that the minister or priest who administered it was later proved to be a rogue or a heretic. Did that render the sacrament useless to the Christian who had received it? Not at all! The work was 'done in the doing', when human need and divine grace came together.

Some Christians still struggle with the whole concept of sacrament. They are so persuaded of the primacy of faith alone as the means of salvation that they deny baptism its sacramental status. Baptism is merely an ordinance, a rite to be administered because Christ commanded it. Among such Christians, including some baptists, the rite of baptism is sometimes optional; unbaptized Christians are not barred from membership or service. Some Christians, most notably Quakers and members of the Salvation Army, dispense with baptism altogether. For Quakers, the inner light is what really matters. In the Salvation Army, faith, often expressed at the penitent form, is sufficient evidence of Christian discipleship.

For the majority of Christians, however, baptism is a sacrament, a sign of sacred reality and a means of grace. Some stress the sacrament more than faith, and others faith more than the sacrament. The two need to be held in creative tension. How that may be done is a question to which this book will return repeatedly.

Confirmation

As has been shown, entry into the church, in the *Didache* as in the New Testament, was a simple affair involving washing in water in the Name of the Father, the Son and the Holy Spirit. By the end of the second century it had become much more complex, involving exorcism, anointing and the laying-on of hands as well as washing with water. Essential to the ceremony was the presence of a bishop.

Once paedobaptism became widespread, however, it frequently became physically impossible for the bishop to preside at all baptisms. Yet because paedobaptism was believed to be imperative, and because many infants died shortly after their birth, the complex initiation rite which was universally called baptism came to be split up. At birth, or as soon as possible thereafter, the infant received the baptism-in-water part of the baptismal ceremony, while the other parts of the ceremony (anointing, laying-on of hands, *etc.*) were given later when the bishop came on his rounds and visited the parish. Two French councils of Riez and Orange in 439 and 441 first called the bishop's ceremonies 'confirmation'. In time, confirmation became a sacrament in its own right, preceding the first communion of the recipient. But it has always struggled to find meaning and significance, for if baptism signifies, among other things, reception of the Holy Spirit, why is a further ceremony necessary?

At the Reformation, Calvin and other leading Reformers appear to have misunderstood the purpose of earlier episcopal visitations, regarding them as times when those baptized in infancy 'confirmed' their baptismal vows and so were fully admitted into the church. They denied confirmation its sacramental status, but retained the rite as a suitable moment for those baptized as infants, now responsibly mature, to express their personal faith in Christ. Problems, however, remained. Was confirmation scriptural, and if so, what was its significance? These and related issues will be discussed later. Suffice to say, among both Catholics and Protestants, confirmation remains a practice seeking a theology and this to the frequent embarrassment of those who encourage and practise it.

Christian sacralism

Sacralism is the view that all the members of a particular state should be bound together by loyalty to the same religion, which then gives political authority to its leaders. Religious dissent then becomes the same as political subversion. For centuries, in antiquity, sacralism bound Roman citizens together in worship of the emperor. That is why Christianity was 'illegal' for so long; Christians refused to acknowledge the Emperor as *dominus et deus*, lord and god.

At the beginning of the fourth century Diocletian was making a last and final systematic attempt to destroy Christianity within the Roman Empire. By the end of the century Christianity had become the Empire's official religion! Now it became as politically subversive not to be Christian as it had been to believe and trust in Jesus Christ. Christian sacralism replaced pagan sacralism as the political and religious creed of Catholic Christianity in east and west.

Not surprisingly, this gave added support to the growing practice of infant baptism because baptism into the church became almost the same as birth into the state. Sacralism survived the Reformation, not only in those nations and states which remained Roman Catholic, but in the Protestant areas which retained state churches as well.

In today's secular world sacralism has lost much of its force as a political and religious creed, although it sometimes continues to be a stumbling block when paedobaptists and baptists try to be reconciled with each other. For, since the fifth century, baptist protest has often been political as well as religious, a cry for freedom from oppressive rulers who have sought divine support for their tyranny, and for freedom from over-powerful religious rulers who have used political force to impose their will on those with whom they have disagreed. We trace the story of some of those medieval baptists, 'protestants' before the Reformation, in chapter five.

Conclusion

At the end of the second century we find Tertullian protesting against infant baptism. For a while, his teaching was heeded. The Emperor Constantine himself delayed his own baptism almost until the end of his life. Many of the church's leading bishops in the fourth and fifth centuries were not baptized until they were adults. If we know about them, how many unknown Christians followed their example?

We need to remember this when, for instance, baptists are sometimes accused of having no history before the Reformation. We shall probably never really know to what extent infant baptism was practised among early Christians, but we do know that for the first three hundred years of the church's life adult baptism was the norm. Even during the fourth century and into the fifth, when paedobaptism was growing in popularity, a counter movement to delay baptism was taking place at the same time. Eventually, in Catholic Christianity, through the influence of Augustine, paedobaptism, as it were, won, and adult baptisms almost came to an end. Even then, those who shared Tertullian's convictions remained in some numbers to protest against the supposedly universal practice of the medieval church.

With the triumph of paedobaptism and the decline of adult baptism went the decline of the Catechumenate, as preparation for baptism was replaced, of necessity, with instruction after baptism. Yet that instruction became increasingly strange to modern ears. For although baptized infants grew up believing that their baptism had brought them forgiveness, eternal life, membership of the church and entry into the family of God, their position in that family became increasingly insecure. In time, at a popular level, a vast system of priests, penances and pilgrimages was needed to preserve their spiritual lives. Even after the intercession of saints, the assistance of Mary, the prayers of the church and the indulgences of the pope, centuries in purgatory still awaited them after death before their souls were cleansed from sin and prepared for heaven.

Christians today may judge for themselves if Tertullian was right to protest against paedobaptism. Of one thing, however, they can be certain. When the specific reasoning of the late second century is stripped from Tertullian's thought, the lines of the ongoing baptismal controversy were laid. Should baptism be a conscious or an unconscious experience? Let children come to baptism, says Tertullian, 'when they are growing up, when they are learning, when they are being taught what they are coming to'. Should baptism reflect some-one's personal accountability to God in the matter of their salvation, or may it be given by others? Let children be made Christians, says Tertullian, 'when they have become competent to know Christ'. In the final analysis, is it baptism in water or faith in Christ which saves? And might not baptism in infancy become a hindrance to faith in maturity? 'Faith unimpaired' by baptism(!), declares Tertullian, 'has no doubt of its salvation.'[20]

References

1. Tertullian, *de baptismo*, I. 5.
2. *ibid*, XVIII. 19-34. Italics ours.
3. In the 1960s the debate was joined in Germany. See Joachim Jeremias, *Infant Baptism in the First Four Centuries* and *The Origins of Infant Baptism* (SCM, 1963), and Kurt Aland, *Did the Early Church Baptize Infants?* (SCM, 1963).
4. See *Didache*, VII. 1-4.
5. See Justin, *First Apology*, 61, 65.
6. See Hippolytus, *Apostolic Tradition*, 21, 22.
7. *Didache*, VII. 1.
8. Justin, *op. cit.*, 61.
9. *Catechetical Lectures of Cyril of Jerusalem*, 9.
10. *Ibid*, 14.
11. Justin, *op. cit.*, 61.
12. Hippolytus, *op. cit.*, 22.
13. Tertullian, *de pudicitia*.
14. Tertullian, *de baptismo*, XVIII.
15. Origen, *Commentary on Romans*, V. ix. 3.
16. Jeremias, *op. cit.* p. 66
17. *Letter of the church of Smyrna*, IX. 3. Quoted in J. Stevenson, *A New Eusebius* (SPCK, 1960), p. 21.
18. See for example, Dom Gregory Dix, *The Theology of Confirmation in Relation to Baptism* (Dacre Press, 1946), p. 31, footnote 2.
19. *The Alternative Service Book 1980*, p. 22.
20. Tertullian, *de baptismo*, XVIII.

5

Medieval Underground

Protest in the West
In the year 1530 a fascinating meeting took place in a Piedmont valley between representatives of two great Christian movements. Leaders of the strange and mysterious Waldensians, called barbes, met ministers of the new Reformed churches of Geneva. The barbes represented a Christian movement which stretched back no-one knew how long; some said to apostolic times. The ministers were in the vanguard of a sweeping new movement which would soon represent Christ in every continent.

The delegates discovered they had many differences. But they agreed heartily on two issues. First, the Catholic Church had forfeited any right to be regarded as the voice of Christianity. Secondly, God was at work in both their movements, drawing men and women to read the Bible, believe the gospel, turn to Christ and live new lives as children of God. Each group went home rejoicing, spreading the good news that the gospel had more witnesses in the past and the present than anyone had suspected. The Reformation had come into contact with the medieval underground!

This useful term covers a multitude of movements, sects and heresies which, throughout the whole of the Middle Ages, gave very varied expression to widespread and indestructible opposition to the Catholic Church. At one time our only sources of information about 'heretics' were the accusations of their persecutors. Now there is a wealth of information available in the records of what they said in their own defence when on trial, and what they taught before they were arrested. What emerges from these is a picture of the Middle Ages that is very different from the one which both Catholics and Protestants have traditionally tended to imagine.

True enough, the Catholic Church had the ear of Europe's leaders and the power of a massive organization. 'It is difficult for us today to imagine the immensity of that power in the Middle Ages ... the Church controlled the sacraments, and the sacraments were essential to salvation.... With these prerogatives in his hand, and the Church at his back, the priest was omnipotent.'[1] But there was always a nagging voice of protest and doubt about this power. The voice was called heresy. Whenever possible it was ignored. If it could not be ignored, its spokesmen were given some concessions and assimilated. If that were not possible, they were maligned, accused and destroyed. Heresy's secret meetings were broken up. A hundred different nicknames were given to its organizations. To a faithful Catholic who troubled to look into the situation continent-wide, heresy must have seemed a hydra-headed monster or a babel of discordant and contradictory beliefs. Yet a closer look revealed an odd sameness in the accusations brought against the heretics.

The Waldensians themselves are an example. Also called Vaudois, Poor Men of Lyons, Vallenses or simply Brethren, their permanent home seems to have been in the high valleys of Switzerland. They were certainly there in the eleventh century, and were still there five hundred years later when the Reformation had begun. But who and what were they? Dissident Catholics enjoying immunity from hostile attention in their remote valleys? Followers of Claudius, Bishop of Turin in the ninth century? Followers of Peter Waldo of Lyons in the twelfth century? What are we to make of the staggering assertion of the Dean of Notre Dame in Arras in the fourteenth century that one-third of Christendom sometimes attended their meetings and was Waldensian at heart?[2] What are we to make of the even more staggering claim they made to the Protestant Reformers that their line of descent could be traced back to the apostles themselves? How could an obscure group of protesters in Switzerland be responsible for a heresy taught everywhere between the Baltic and the Mediterranean? Was the word Waldensian in fact just a convenient label for any dissenting sect? Probably so. 'In 1184 Waldensianism began its long history as a sectarian movement, spreading throughout central Europe and absorbing in different regions the local heresies in ever new combinations.'[3]

To regard medieval heresy as one distinguishable and uniform movement would be a gross over-simplification. Protestants have sometimes been tempted in this direction. In reply to the Catholic boast of one unchanging church in every century, periodic Protestant attempts have been made to trace a 'thin red line' of witness through every century too. Such attempts have provided their supporters with some embarrassing bedfellows whose only common factor was a dislike of Rome and all her ways. 'Dissent' and 'protest' would perhaps be more accurate titles of the medieval underground than either 'evangelicalism' or 'heresy'.[4] Some of the movements were in fact heretical. All were deeply medieval. Some could fairly be called protestant and evangelical.

Certainly some themes constantly reappear in the heresy trials. Protest groups condemned the 'worldliness' of the official church, rejected its priestly system, regarded its sacraments with suspicion and sought a biblical simplicity of religious life. But of course all of these issues raised problems with baptism, which was administered to infants for the washing away of original sin where the church was in power, and administered *en masse* to whole regions on the borders of Christendom when some local king or ruler embraced the Catholic faith. Searching questions were asked. If the church is hopelessly corrupt, what of the validity of its baptisms? If priestcraft and sacramentalism are to be rejected, should baptism be rejected too? Is a call to personal commitment consistent with a baptism indiscriminately applied? Various answers were given, for many disconnected 'heresies' were involved, but generally speaking, 'salvation by believing response to the preached Word and salvation by sacramental manipulation, lay in mortal combat with each other all through medieval times'.[5]

The Waldenses or Waldensians are the only medieval sect unequivocally recognized among modern Protestants as holding the same faith as themselves. When, as we have seen, Swiss Reformers met Waldensian leaders, there was mutual delight. 'The Waldensians provided the early Protestants with a splendid riposte to the question, "Where was your church before Luther?"'[6]

Caught up in the Reformation, the Waldensians evolved from a rather amorphous 'movement' into a modern 'church' which is the strongest Protestant denomination in Italy to this day. Nowadays their claims to antiquity are modest. They trace their undoubted history back to the eleventh century, and speak in general terms of links with earlier movements. Their progress in the Middle Ages was chequered. At times they were content to be a ginger group within Catholicism, working hopefully for reform, and for the sake of safety accepting Catholic sacraments with a secret mental reservation. Calvin would later scorn this as 'Nicodemism', but that was rather unfair. The atti-

tude arose, not from cowardice, but from a deeply 'inward and spiritual' view of worship and faith. Rightly or wrongly, they simply
dismissed enforced visible sacraments as an unwelcome but irrelevant fact of life which did the soul neither good nor harm.[7]

At other times the Waldensians adopted an almost monastic policy.
Indeed Peter Waldo, their first undisputed leader, bore a strong re-
semblance to Francis of Assisi (whom he preceded by thirty years).
The hesitant papal approval given to the Franciscans was only just
denied to the 'Poor Men of Lyons' whom Peter Waldo led. Yet at
other times Waldensians were a much more recognizably evangelistic movement, and more than once before and after the Reformation
experienced what can only be described as an evangelical awakening.

Not surprisingly, then, Waldensian attitudes to baptism were not
always the same. One scholar maintains, 'Infant Baptism was widely
regarded as desirable for salvation',[8] while another asserts, 'The Baptism of believers by immersion was common to the Waldenses'.[9]

The truth seems to be that the Waldensians practised paedobaptism
quite widely among their own children. In the remote Alpine valleys
where the movement always survived whatever its fortunes elsewhere,
whole communities were Waldensian, and it was virtually certain that
children born among them would maintain the faith in adult life. But
when Catholics were converted to their movement, they 'rebaptized'
them, for they were conceived as turning from the false church to the
true. This seems to indicate that they were opposed to Catholic baptism
rather than to infant baptism. It was an attitude which was later to
irritate Martin Luther when he came across it – especially when they
cheerfully applied the same policy to Lutherans! 'They baptize little
ones ... and rebaptize those who come to them from us,' he
complained.[10]

'What the Waldensians had against "christening" was not the infancy of the recipient, but the Constantinian overtones of the ritual.
Therefore they rebaptized converts from the prevailing Church and
practised infant baptism in the case of their own little ones.'[11]   Here,
then, is an example of a respectable 'Protestant' movement, which
had a dual approach to paedobaptism and believers' baptism.

Light in the East

In contrast to the Waldensians are the Paulicians. They survived and sometimes flourished on the eastern borders of Europe, and had a similar relationship with the Orthodox Church to that of Waldensianism with Rome. Their stance was one of more open opposition, and they aroused corresponding anger. They endured merciless persecution, and sometimes responded by taking up arms. With cheerful impartiality these were accused of being 'Manichaeans' and 'Mohammedans', and it is not easy to decide just what in fact they were. Clearly the worst accusations were quite unjustified, and as with all investigations into the beliefs of the medieval underground, it must be assumed that those who did not scruple to murder them would not hesitate to malign them.

Their origins went far back beyond the Middle Ages – certainly as far as the sixth century in Asia Minor. They insistently maintained that they represented not a heresy, nor even a reform movement, but a primitive form of Christianity which had resisted the innovations of Orthodoxy. As late as 1828, a colony of their survivors settled in Armenia and brought an ancient manual of doctrine, allegedly dating back for a thousand years. It was translated into English seventy years later as *The Key of Truth* and created a sensation. They were hailed as 'Ancient Oriental Baptists ... in many respects Protestants before Protestantism'.[12]

More recently, scholars are inclined to be a little less enthusiastic, especially about the Paulician doctrine of Christ, and a modern dictionary describes them more cautiously as 'an evangelical antihierarchical sect originating in the seventh century ... whose characteristic doctrines include Adoptionist Christology, the Authority of Scripture ... and Believers' Baptism'.[13] 'There are three divine mysteries which God proclaimed,' wrote the author of *The Key of Truth*. 'First, repentance; second, baptism; third, holy communion. These three He gave to the adults and not to catechumens who have not repented or are unbelieving.'[14]

The Paulician convert, or the Paulician child grown to maturity, was baptized in a kneeling position in the water of any convenient river. He confessed his past sin and present faith 'with love and tears' as he knelt in the water, '...and then as he that has believed completes his holy profession of faith, the elect one (that is, the minister) instantly takes the water into his hands, and looking up to heaven ...

shall empty out the water over the head, saying: In the Name of the Father and Son and Holy Spirit is baptized this man or woman, by the testimony of the congregation here present.'[15]

The Paulician approach to Orthodox Christianity was one of radical protest. They regarded the use of icons and holy pictures and the dependence on priests and sacraments as the invasion of Christianity by pagan customs. Significantly they maintained that one of the principal causes of this invasion was precisely the enforced baptism of still semi-pagan adults and the baptism of infants incapable of faith. Non-Christian habits and thought-forms, they maintained, were thus bound to creep in to the churches. There can be little doubt that the Paulicians taught Adoptionism, that most persistent and attractive of Christological heresies from which few Christian movements have been completely immune.[16] This lessens the value of their witness in some respects, but does not diminish the interest and importance of their approach to baptism. We can read of their objections to baptizing 'the unbelieving, the reasonless, and the unrepentant'. It must be remembered that at that early stage the indiscriminate, and even enforced, baptism of adult pagans was commonplace on the frontiers of Christendom. However, any form of paedobaptism was banned by them. For the children of Paulician believers there was prescribed a moving service of thanksgiving, parental vows, naming and prayerful dedication. Baptism itself was administered only to those who 'earnestly sought' it – another indication that believers' baptism, not merely adult baptism, was in mind. Many Paulicians preferred to delay baptism until the age of thirty, so as to resemble Christ more closely. They linked the descent of the Holy Spirit upon Jesus at Jordan with his own awareness of his unique relationship with the Father, and with the Christian's awareness of adoption into the family of God. It was this emphasis that led them onto thin ice in their Christology – a fact which the Orthodox were quick to grasp and to exploit.

The medieval underground was a complex phenomenon, and must be approached with caution in support of an argument. Yet we shall see its successor during and after the Reformation, and hear far-off echoes of its voice in modern movements. From the point of view of this book it underlines one point: that people's attitude towards Christendom in general and baptism in particular will be shaped by the state of religion as they find it. In their situation, the medieval 'heretics' tended to see paedobaptism as a representative sacrament of superstition and worldly religion. In contrast, adult baptism came to represent salvation by faith, protest against corrupt Christendom, and suffering for the sake of purified religion.

The situation today may be very different, but the questions they posed and only partially answered, are still with us.

References

1. H. Wheeler Robinson, *Baptist Principles* (Carey Kingsgate Press, 1935), p. 46.
2. Leonard Verduin, *The Reformers and Their Stepchildren* (Paternoster Press, 1964), p. 173.
3. G. H. Williams, *The Radical Reformation* (Weidenfield & Nicholson, 1962), p. 520.
4. As, for example, in Jeffery Burton, *Dissent and Reform in the Early Middle Ages* (Cambridge University Press, 1968).
5. Verduin, *op. cit.*, p. 153.
6. *The New International Dictionary of the Christian Church* (Paternoster Press, 1974), p. 1026.
7. See Williams, *op. cit.*, p. 578, for a full discussion.
8. *Ibid.*, p. 526.
9. E. H. Broadbent, *The Pilgrim Church* (Pickering & Inglis, 1935), p. 130.
10. Verduin, *op. cit.*, p. 196.
11. *Ibid.*
12. E. C. Adeney, *The Greek and Eastern churches.* Quoted in Robinson, *Baptist Principles*, p. 59.
13. *The New International Dictionary of the Christian Church*, p. 755.
14. *The Key of Truth*, p. 116f. Quoted in Robinson, *op. cit.*, p. 59.
15. *Ibid.*, p. 60.
16. Adoptionism is the view that Jesus was a man of blameless life who became the adoptive Son of God.

6

Reformation Tragedy

One bitterly cold January day in 1527 a boat on the River Limmat was carrying a man to his death. At his trial Felix Manz had freely confessed to being a teacher of doctrines forbidden in Switzerland: 'We bring together those who are willing to accept Christ, obey the Word, and follow in His footsteps. We unite them by baptism, and leave the rest to their present conviction.'[1] Pressed to enlarge on his views about baptism in particular, he admitted: 'More is involved in Baptism: things on which I prefer not to enlarge just now.'[2] The Clerk of Courts wrote an explanatory comment in the records: 'They do not allow Infant Baptism. In this way they will put an end to secular authority.'[3]

What an extraordinary comment! More extraordinary still is the outburst of his accuser Ulrich Zwingli, Switzerland's heroic Protestant Reformer. Speaking of men like Manz he cried, 'Let him who talks about going under [the water] go under.'[4] To the authorities it seemed poetic justice. Felix Manz was condemned to death by drowning.

Led into the boat, he was forced to sit up and his arms were passed around his bent knees and bound at the wrists. Next a stick was pushed between knees and elbows to secure him in this position. The boat was rowed to the centre of the river, and the helpless prisoner was thrown overboard, to choke in the dark, deep waters.

Protestant had killed Protestant for the crime of obeying God's Word as they understood it. How could so strange a thing happen, just ten years after the beginning of the Reformation in Europe? It happened because the Reformation of the sixteenth century rediscovered the New Testament gospel, but failed to recreate the New Testament church.

To say this is not to belittle the achievement of the great Reformers: Luther, Zwingli, Calvin and their colleagues. What they did was astonishing. The world was permanently changed by their endeavours. The Christian gospel of the early centuries, buried under a mountain of medieval priestcraft and superstition, was unearthed and revealed again as the good news of the free grace of God, offered directly to men and women in Jesus Christ.

Taught by the rediscovered Scriptures, interpreted by the Holy Spirit, and worked out agonizingly in their own experience, this gospel first transformed the Reformers themselves. It gave them the courage to withstand powerful adversaries, the clarity to dismiss centuries of tradition and the conviction which enabled them to win the attention of multitudes. To acknowledge this is only just. But to deny that their efforts contained an element of error and confusion is to deny that they were human at all.

The facts are plain. The Reformers found the gospel and preached it with immense effect to the conversion of many. In so doing, they destroyed the framework of medieval Christendom. But when they were required to replace that framework and to cater for those converts, they faltered and became confused and divided. The division of Protestantism into Lutheran, Calvinistic and Anglican forms shows this. The later subdivision of Calvinism into Presbyterian, Independent and Baptist denominations underlines it further. But the most convincing evidence is provided by the story of the tragic conflict which developed between the main-line Protestants and the Anabaptists. In that conflict the issue of baptism was raised, sometimes came close to being resolved, but eventually drove two parties into irreconcilable collision. As a result, the progress of the Reformation ground to a halt for a generation. As a further result, it has been argued, Protestantism lost the working-classes of Europe.

The Anabaptists of the sixteenth century present us with perplexing problems. The word means 're-baptizers'. Its use pinpoints two features held in common by a large number of separate radical movements. They all condemned the Reformation as half-hearted and incomplete. They all rejected paedobaptism, and baptized or rebaptized only those who came to a decisive experience of religious commitment. The same two things could be said of twentieth-century Pentecostals, Baptists, Brethren, House Churches, Christadelphians, Mormons and Jehovah's Witnesses. To class all of these, orthodox and heretical, under the name Baptist is about as accurate and fair as to class all the sixteenth-century radicals together as Anabaptists. Political revolutionaries and anti-trinitarian mystics were lumped together in popular thinking with simple evangelical believers who wished to take the Reformation to what they believed to be its scriptural and logical conclusion. Some of them were converts of the Reformers. Others were survivors from the persecuted but persistent 'medieval underground'.

Today the Anabaptists are known by various names (the Reformation Radicals, the Second Front, the Reformers' Stepchildren, the Common Man's Reformers, *etc.*) and their moving story is only being revealed and understood as scholars unearth and interpret what they wrote about themselves, rather than what was often unjustly written about them. Once regarded with embarrassment as fanatics from the lunatic fringe of Christendom, they are now increasingly recognized as part of a movement which had genuine Christian strands, and whose witness carries a challenge for our day. The British writer who has most painstakingly collected and analysed their writings says, 'Christians of many denominations are finding themselves ... closer to the despised sectaries of the Reformation Era than to the classical defenders of a reformed corpus christianum.'[5]

Basically, the Anabaptists were asking for regenerate church membership. For a thousand years, they said, state and church had been in an alliance foreign to the nature of the gospel. As part of that alliance, baptism had become 'christening' – the artificial christianizing of a whole population. But now that the true nature of the gospel had been rediscovered, it was possible to break the false structure and return to the New Testament pattern – believers gathered together in voluntary association, whose government and sacraments were of no concern to political power.

This is now generally acknowledged to be the basic tenet of the most Christian of the Anabaptist groups. As the church historian Latourette says, Anabaptism was 'a manifestation of a continuing strain in Christianity which had been present from the very beginning, and which, before and since the Reformation, has expressed itself in many forms'.[6]

Interestingly, baptism became the visible and verbal centre of the controversy. But, as so often before and since, the visible rite of baptism only focused a deeper and wider debate. This is the tragic significance of the story.

Martin Luther
Much in the teaching of the Radicals followed logically enough from Martin Luther's own teaching, and in the early years he was very

much attracted to them. In his own groping for the light, he had found in himself only the depths of sin, in God only an inexorable justice, and in the church only a paraphernalia of sacraments and sacerdotalism which gave him no peace with God. Through studying the Bible with desperate intensity, he had come gradually to understand that 'the righteousness of God' means, not God's anger at sin, but his willingness to declare the sinner pardoned, acquitted, justified, out of sheer love. To achieve this, the Father had delivered up his Son to suffer the consequences of men's sin. By his Spirit he now brings the sinner to repentance, faith, pardon, acceptance and sonship. What no amount of religious observance or moral effort could achieve, became freely available to those who abandoned themselves in faith to the Christ preached in the gospel.

This was Luther's great discovery. Easily, it could have led him to the conclusion that only those who thus believe and find assurance belong to the church, and that they should meet together as believers on the ground of that assurance. He nearly came to that position. In 1523, before the Anabaptists had emerged, and when the first stage of the Reformation was in full swing, he said, 'My intention is, in days to come, not to admit any when communion is held, save such as have been interviewed and have given suitable answers as to their personal faith. The rest would be excluded.'[7]

This, however, was very much a vision for some possible future date. For Luther must not be thought of as a master-planner with every move anticipated and with a clear view of his goal. He was simply caught up in tremendous events and continually had to improvise. In 1517 when his voice first sounded in protest and the world woke up to his presence, he had no thoughts of destroying the Catholic Church. It was the only church he knew. Within its fold he had eventually discovered the gospel. Within its organization he had preached that gospel for two years. He wished only to draw the church's attention to the implications of that gospel on abuses which were sullying its life. And in 1517 one of the most flagrant abuses made him speak out: the selling of 'indulgences'[8] for cash; the solemn assurance that, 'as soon as the coin in the coffer rings, the soul from purgatory springs'.[9]

From then onwards Luther gradually realized how deep and bitter the conflict was to be. In 1516 he was simply rejoicing in an experience of God's forgiveness. In 1517 he wished to apply his experience

to the abuse of indulgences. In 1518 he believed the Pope to be mistaken, but hoped to enlighten him. By 1519 he believed that general
councils of the historic church could be in grave error. By 1520 he
concluded that the papacy was the great beast of the Apocalypse, due
to be destroyed by the wrath of God.

But, by that time, Luther was reorganising Catholic parish churches
wherever his influence was felt, so that gradually the shape of the
Lutheran church appeared. Here a liturgy would be changed; there an
emphasis would be altered; in another place a superstition was quietly
buried. The framework was there, and Luther and his colleagues
worked away at its adaptation to more evangelical principles as they
were hammered out on the anvil of experience and controversy. But
the framework was there: a framework of state-supported churches,
established by law in areas where all were considered to be Christians
in some sense, and where the life of the church was one side of the
life of the state.

In fact, two different things were happening, and the two would
eventually collide. The Reformation had a popular following of
ordinary folk who were enlightened and enthused by evangelical
preaching, plus members of the old persecuted sects who found a
national leader suddenly saying more or less what they had always
believed. At the same time, the Reformation had the support of
authority: local princes who, for a mixture of religious, political and
personal motives, supported Luther's quarrel with Rome and permitted
him to influence the churches which came under their control.

What course, then, was Luther to follow? The increasingly bellig-
erent answer of the enthusiasts was 'Scrap everything and start again.
Leave the churches. Preach the gospel, baptize the converts, and gather
them together for fellowship, breaking of bread and prayers.' The
increasing pressure of events said, 'Tread carefully: a false move,
and you lose the ear of Europe and find yourself leader of just another
persecuted sect. Keep the framework and deal patiently and graciously
with the people within it. Gradually remove abuses when people are
ready to be rid of them. Recapture Christendom for Christ, parish
churches, priests, princes and all.' But to abandon paedobaptism meant
to abandon the whole church organization and at the same time knock
away its foundations.

'Consider what disruption would ensue if there should develop
among us two categories, the baptized and the unbaptized,' said

Luther's friend, Melanchthon. 'If baptism were to be discontinued
for most people, an openly pagan way of life would come about.'[10]
That was precisely the problem. The baptism of only consciously
committed Christians seemed incompatible with the rebuilding of a
reformed Christendom and the establishing of Christian nations. 'Precisely so,' said the enthusiasts. 'But who cares about rebuilding Christendom? The idea is a delusion anyway. Neither the word nor the
idea is to be found in the New Testament. The sooner it is forgotten
the better. Uncommitted people are pagans, whether they live in Germany or in China. Then why not say so?'

This was the real baptismal controversy. Both the fascination and
the tragedy of the Reformation from this point arises from the fact
that the problem was not resolved, and that equally earnest Christians
moved gradually from two positions very close together, to two positions hopelessly opposed. Brothers in Christ who began by discuss-
ing together over their Bibles, finished by literally killing each other.

Ulrich Zwingli

The sad story can perhaps be followed more clearly at Zurich than at
Wittenberg. The proudly independent Swiss, with their self-ruling
cities and powerful city councils, found their own way into a Reformed
Christianity. In 1518 a young Catholic clergyman called Ulrich
Zwingli was appointed 'people's priest' or 'common preacher' to the
great cathedral at Zurich. He had just come through a period of spiritual
struggle to a personal faith in Christ. In his very first sermon he
announced to the startled congregation: 'It is to Christ I wish to lead
you. He is the source of salvation. His Gospel is the power of God to
all that believe.'[11] His powerful and popular preaching, which took
the form of vivid expositions of Scripture, forcefully applied, gave
the impression that 'a man from the apostolic age was standing before
you'.[12]

During the next five years reforms were gradually introduced in
Zurich, and then in other Swiss cities, by what became the character-
istically Zwinglian method: first evangelistic preaching, then a public debate arranged by the city council, finally a reform adopted and
decreed by the council. In five years the churches were distinctively
'Protestant' with an evangelicalism more simple and more radical
than that of the Lutheran churches. With the enthusiastic support of
growing numbers of clergy, laity and city councillors, images were

removed, the mass abolished, clergy permitted to marry and relics banished. By 1525 the churches of Switzerland had unequivocally broken with Rome.

At that very time the Anabaptist controversy developed. Zwingli had given baptism much thought. 'Nothing grieves me more than that at present I must baptize children, for I know it ought not to be done.'[13] But his position was difficult. His office in the cathedral, which he employed with devastating effect, was held by arrangement with the civic authorities. Slowly but surely (more surely than the church authorities!) they were defending his action, accepting his reforms and giving effect to them. 'But if I were to stop the practice of Infant Baptism, I would lose my office.'[14]

To call this cowardice would be unjust. With fearless courage Zwingli defied every convention and every authority when once he became convinced that a reform was necessary for the sake of the gospel. He did not consider this to be such a case:

'I leave baptism untouched. I call it neither right nor wrong. If we were to baptize as Christ instituted it, then we would not baptize any person until he reached the years of discretion, for I find Infant Baptism nowhere written or practised. But we must practise it now so as not to offend our fellow men .... It is better not to preach (adult baptism) until the world is ready to receive it.'[15]

Unfortunately, while the world was still unready to receive it, there were men in the church eager to practise it! Conrad Grebel was one of Zwingli's converts. By 1523 he was chafing at the slowness of his leadership in reform. By 1524 he had come to his own conclusion about baptism and church membership. Rejecting paedobaptism, he was gathering an informal group of converted and enthusiastic people for worship and teaching. Known popularly as 'Swiss Brethren', they became a church-within-the-church, and then a separate movement. Both Zwingli and the civil authorities were embarrassed by them, and in January 1525 the city council ordered them to disband their movement and particularly to desist from 'rebaptizing'. Grebel refused to do so, and after an evangelistic trip around Switzerland in which he won many converts, he was imprisoned, escaped and died in hiding two years later.

By this time another leader had appeared. Balthasar Hubmaier, a Catholic priest and an opponent of Luther, had a dramatic conversion.

The two influences which led to this were Lutheranism and the teaching of the 'Bohemian Brethren', survivors of the 'medieval underground'. The latter taught baptism for believers only and (unusually for that time) by immersion. Hubmaier came to accept this position, and after thoroughly evangelising his own parish in Waldshut, he baptized three hundred members of his parish church. Shortly after, the tide of war lapped over that region, and he fled into Switzerland and settled in Zurich. Having just silenced one troublesome sectarian, Zwingli now found himself saddled with another! The city council, still troubled about the whole thing, arranged a public disputation, after first imprisoning and torturing Hubmaier.

The exchange was heated. Hubmaier accused Zwingli of inconsistency. He knew of the Reformer's earlier doubts. 'You used to hold the same ideas. Hundreds of people have heard it from your mouth.' Zwingli had to assert that he had been mistaken: 'Rashly accepting that the sign testifies to the faith, we had to attack infant baptism ... This error misled me.'[16] In other words he had now made up his mind that baptism did not need to be an expression of the conscious faith of the person baptized: it was a sign of God's promises, not man's acceptance of them. Moreover, he had turned his face from any idea of a separated group of believers, and settled for a continuation of the policy of reforming Christendom from within.

The council felt the same. They had already warned the Reformer not to take his teachings to such extremes that the state-church alliance was broken: 'Then there would spring up disobedience towards the magistrates, disunity, heresy, and the weakening and diminution of the Christian faith.'[17]

The council now issued another edict which threatened banishment to all who refused to have their children baptized. Zwingli went into print with a sustained attack on the troublemakers. His tract *Of Baptism* introduced what Calvin would later develop as a 'covenant argument' for infant baptism, but also warned, 'The issue is not baptism, but revolt, faction, heresy.'[18] The leaders of the Radicals fled the country, to scatter their teaching throughout Europe and to face martyrdom within two years.

The Reformers and the zealots
The Reformation leaders now took a grim step. They believed that an abyss was opening up at their feet. They were mocked by the Catholics

who jeered, 'We told you so – you have torn apart the seamless robe of Christ. Tear it in two pieces and soon it will be in a hundred fragments.' They were harassed by anxious authorities who warned of the collapse of civil order. They were horrified by the extremes of the wilder fanatics, for when the demands of enthusiasts are refused, they become not less extreme but more. And the outbreak of the Peasants' War in Germany (a popular uprising of aggrieved artisans, quickly crushed) convinced them that their worst fears were really justified. Order was in danger of disappearing and Anabaptism worsened the danger. First Zwingli and then Luther invoked the help of the civil power against the Anabaptists. Using the weapons of imprisonment and banishment, they found that the first only created sympathy and the second only scattered sectarianism more widely. The fateful decision was taken to make 'heresy' a capital offence. Beheading, burning or drowning became the regular punishments for preaching the Radical faith.

Naturally enough, the Radicals reacted. From admiring but chiding the Protestant leaders, they turned to condemning them as antichrist. Members of Anabaptist sects were forbidden to enter a Protestant church building. Any hope of mutual understanding and accommodation was lost. Attitudes about baptism hardened. Several groups had never been totally against paedobaptism but were only opposed to its indiscriminate application to the children of those whom they felt to be unbelievers. Now the gap widened. All paedobaptism came to mean to them 'christening' – the weapon of a fallen church and a discredited Christendom. On the other hand, adult baptism came to mean more than a personal act of obedience and loyalty; it became an eloquent way of rejecting Christian sacralism and all it stood for. 'It became principally a matter of separation for the purpose of creating a divided church. Their leaders receive baptism as a sign of separation ... and the wish to abandon the Papists and the Lutherans,'[19] wrote Henry Bullinger, Luther's successor. 'Live as Christ-like as you please. Only desist from re-baptizing, for it is as plain as day that with it you are making a faction,'[20] cried Zwingli.

The accusation was a just one, and the Anabaptists cheerfully admitted it. 'The medieval order can be laid low in no more effective way than by abolishing infant baptism,'[21] claimed Conrad Grebel. 'Infant Baptism is a supporting pillar of the papal order. As long as it is not removed, there can be no Christian congregation,'[22] agreed Hans

Sockler, and by 'the papal order' he meant Christendom, whether Catholic or Protestant. 'They fight for Infant Baptism, not out of love for children... but in order that they may hold up a false Christendom... which is the abomination of desolation,'[23] wrote another bitterly. The number of imprisonments and executions is impossible to estimate, but in whole areas very popular movements were extinguished, that had the sympathy and support of the common people.

Not surprisingly, the expectation of suffering became an essential part of Anabaptist teaching, and baptism itself took on a further deep meaning. Not only was it a demonstration of the convert's desire to 'die to self', but it was also a likely route to literal death, or at any rate to physical suffering. Conrad Grebel wrote, combining both thoughts:

> 'He that is baptized has been planted into the death of Christ. True Christians are sheep among wolves, ready for the slaughter. They must be baptized into anguish and affliction, tribulation, persecution, suffering and death. They must be tried in the fire, and must reap the fatherland of rest, not by killing their bodily enemies but by mortifying their spiritual enemies.'[24]

We should not imagine that the Reformers themselves now simply relied on civil persecution to settle the issue. They were embarrassed and grieved, and they struggled to meet the Anabaptists' arguments at the higher level of theological debate. Martin Luther worked out a threefold answer to the Anabaptist case. He classified his own doctrine of paedobaptism. He worked out a theology of the church. And he pursued the idea of *ecclesiola in ecclesia* – a faithful church within the wider church (literally 'a little church within the church').

Luther's great book *The Babylonian Captivity of the Church* dealt with the subject of the Sacraments. He utterly repudiated the Catholic idea of *ex opere operato*.[25] Anything which contradicted the basic principle of 'God's grace offered in the Word and received by Faith' was ruthlessly rejected. The Catholic sacraments of penance, matrimony, ordination, extreme unction and confirmation were denied sacramental status at all. Christ had ordained two sacraments for the church: baptism and communion. Communion was cut free from the traditional mass which made it a life-giving miracle dependent upon a priestly act. Luther linked it firmly to faith: it declares the grace of God in the giving of Christ and both stirs up and responds to the faith of the communicant. To this he added a difficult conception of the glorified body of Christ present in every place, and on this issue fell out with Zwingli.

But what of baptism? This too Luther linked with faith. What justifies the recipient is not the baptism, but faith in the promises of God which are associated with baptism. Those incapable of believing, such as infants, are assisted by the faith of those who bring them to baptism and by the prayers of the Christians who are witnesses. Faith would then be expected to make its appearance in the growing child's developing experience. Moreover, when adult years are reached, the Christian must continually 'carry out his baptism' by dying to sin, and by living in a daily attitude of dependence on Christ.

Luther made the baptismal service an impressive one, which included acts of exorcism, the sign of the cross, the use of salt and the immersion of the child in water. Later he was attracted to the extraordinary proposition that the infant does in fact exercise faith. Insisting rightly enough that saving faith means much more than *fides* ('I give my mental assent') and is *fiducia* ('I surrender myself in trust'), he asserted as Reformed Christianity always has done since, that such faith is itself a gift of God. 'Right faith is a thing wrought by the Holy Ghost in us, which changeth us and turneth us into a new nature. How then can we insist that we know exactly when faith is granted?' he asked. 'We hopefully assume the child to be a believer and thus regenerate. The baptism then strengthens the seed of faith. Daily the sinner drowns the sinful man within him by the renewal of his baptismal vows.'[26]

'Luther thought that Infant Baptism best expressed the true relationship of the sinner to God in the matter of salvation. The helpless child symbolised how the grace of God alone saves man ... Since he believed that man, in matters of faith was absolutely helpless even as an adult, that it was a divine miracle ... it was not difficult for him to accept Infant Baptism.'[27]

But in the long run, as Luther himself explained, 'We bring the child with the conviction and the hope that it will come to faith, and we pray that God will give it faith. But we do not baptize on the strength of this belief, but wholly on the fact that God has commanded it.' He was prepared to leave it at that.[28]

Luther could not have been very happy with his own rather complicated conclusions on this subject. They show him at his worst, as his magnificently truculent teaching about the nature of faith, the authority of Scripture and the victory of Christ, show him at his best. On the whole, his baptismal teaching has not commended itself to his successors, and is not typical of Protestant thinking. More effective was his doctrine of the church.

Luther's doctrine of the church
This, as he realized, was the real issue with the Anabaptists, just as the doctrine of salvation was the real issue with the Catholics. What then is the church? First, he asserted that it most certainly is not the papacy. The claim of the church of Rome to be the one universal and apostolic church was rejected with derision. It had neither preserved the gospel nor imitated the way of life exemplified by the apostles. Secondly, he saw the logic of his own rediscovery of the gospel as the message of salvation received by faith. If the church is to guard, express and propagate that gospel, it must be made up of those who embrace its truths. This led him into difficulties.

Luther understood clearly that the true church, known only to God, must consist of all those (and only those) who are genuine believers. Could this be expressed in any visible manner? 'The right kind of evangelical order cannot be exhibited among all sorts of people. But those who are determined to be Christians... must enrol themselves by name and meet apart for prayer and reading, to baptize and take the sacrament,' he wrote. 'But I have not yet the right people for it.'[29] Precisely! The parish churches as he knew them were full of people making a greater or lesser response to the new understanding of the gospel.

Luther's solution was to place the critical emphasis on the visible order and profession of the church. Thus, wherever the gospel is truly preached and the sacraments are scripturally observed and people with good intentions are hearing the preaching and receiving the sacraments, the church is present and functioning, and 'we cannot question that among the mass of people, God has His own little group of true believers, few or many'.[30]

The way in which such churches were to be organized was as *Landeskirchen* – territorial churches. The convictions of the majority in a given area were to determine the universal practice in that area, established by law, and presenting a united front. Those who differed should move to an area where the beliefs of the majority were more acceptable to them. This startling proposition was in fact a possibility in sixteenth-century Europe with its multiplicity of small provinces and city states. Successive areas declared for or against the Reformation and, until the religious wars broke out, their declarations were generally accepted.

This then was Luther's doctrine of the church. He was perfectly aware that it held a tension within itself. Sometimes he accepted that as inevitable; the tension between ideal and reality. At other times he was depressed and discouraged by its outworking, and irritably envious of the admittedly higher standards adopted by the Anabaptists. Was the choice always to be between a too-inclusive church which compromised its own witness and a too-exclusive church which offered little room for the weak? As a middle way, he pursued a further idea, often referred to as *ecclesiola in ecclesia*. This was an attempt to gather together within the wider church those members who showed convincing signs of true conversion and spiritual growth.

Luther groped after some system in which true believers among the mass of nominal Lutherans could assemble in private houses as well as gather in the larger congregations, and wondered if a more meaningful observation of communion and baptism might be possible in the private gatherings alone. He even toyed with the idea of separating church congregations into two groups, with a minister teaching the convinced Christians in the cloister while a chaplain addressed the majority in the church!

As the gap between Lutherans and Radicals widened, these ideas were shelved, but they are thoughts to which members of 'state churches' have often returned. The most striking example is the birth of the 'societies' in eighteenth-century Anglicanism, which were the seed-beds of Methodism.

This, then, was Luther's reply to the Radical challenge. A deeply spiritual view of the true church was combined with a realistic acceptance of the actual situation in Christendom. Faith was pinned to a process of patient teaching and reform. But with it went a dependence upon political powers and geographical organizations. The Radicals were not impressed. Abused and tormented, they continued on their own path of separation and restitution. Scattered and disorganized, they fragmented into a multiplicity of sects. Robbed by death of their best leaders, they sometimes followed fanatics. With little chance of peacefully developing a coherent theology, some drifted into heresy. Thus one wing of the Reformation began to slow down and set in a rigid and worldly position, while the other was in danger of being destroyed by persecution or discredited by fanaticism.

That both dangers were eventually to be avoided was due largely to two remarkable men who now appeared. Each faced the issue of church and baptism. Each made a different response. Each offered a distinctive contribution to the debate. Each has left a mark on every successive generation. Their names are Menno Simons and John Calvin.

References

1. Leonard Verduin, *The Reformers and Their Stepchildren* (Paternoster Press, 1964), p. 74.
2. *Quellen zur Geschichte der Taufer in der Schweiz*, p. 51. (A German collection of original sources of Reformation material, hereafter called *Quellen.*)
3. Verduin, *op. cit.*, 205.
4. *Ibid.*, p. 217. The books by Verduin and Williams have brought a mass of documentation to the attention of English-speaking readers, and have led to a drastic reconsideration in recent times of the Anabaptist movement. Williams' work is more detailed and comprehensive, but we have usually quoted Verduin, who writes in a simpler and more popular style.
5. G. H. Williams, *The Radical Reformation* (Weidenfield & Nicholson, 1962), p. 31.
6. Kenneth Scott Latourette, *A History of Christianity* (Eyre & Spottiswoode, 1954; see bibliography for new edition), p. 786.
7. Written in a letter to Luther's friend Nicholas Haussman. Quoted in Verduin, *op. cit.*, p. 127.
8. Indulgences' – remission of punishment still due for sin after sacramental absolution, granted after gifts of money to the church.
9. Roland Bainton, *Here I Stand* (Lion Publishing, 1983), p. 78. Many other editions.
10. Philip Melancthon, *Works*, Vol. 20.
11. D. W. Marshall, 'Approaches to the reformation of the church', *Evangelical Magazine* (special report), December 1965.
12. *Quellen*, 6, p. 184.
13. Verduin, *op. cit.*, p. 198.
14. *Ibid.*, p. 199.
15. *Quellen*, 9, p. 186.

16. Verduin, *op. cit.*, p. 201f.
17. *Ibid.*
18. Williams, *op. cit.*, p. 131.
19. *Corpus reformatorum*, Vol. 91, p. 246.
20. Quoted in Verduin, *op. cit.*, p. 205.
21. *Ibid.*
22. *Mennonite Quarterly Review*, Vol. 21 (1947), p. 283.
23. E. H. Broadbent, *The Pilgrim Church* (Pickering & Inglis, 1935), p. 275.
24. Verduin, *op. cit.*, p. 260.
25. Verduin, *op. cit.*, p. 262
26. Knaake (ed.), *Works of Martin Luther* (Muhlenburg Press for Concordia, 1960), Vol. 30, p. 448.
27. *Ibid.*, p. 476.
28. *Ibid.*, p. 449
29. Broadbent, *op. cit.*, p. 148.
30. *Ibid.*

7

Mennonites and Calvinists

Menno Simons

In 1524 a twenty-eight-year-old Catholic priest was appointed to the curacy of a Dutch church. His name was Menno Simons, and he was destined to do more than any other single man for the survival of the Anabaptists and their recovery from the perils of fanaticism.

He was a thoroughly worldly cleric of the type so common at that time. More interested in drinking and gambling than in the nominal discharge of his duties, he was nevertheless aware of the religious turmoil around him. During Menno's training and ordination, Luther had been thundering his denunciations of the papacy and flooding Europe with his evangelical pamphlets. The general air of questioning and unease affected the newly consecrated priest, and he resolved to avoid reading the Bible 'fearing that if I read I might be misled'.[1] His unease persisted, and within a year he found himself doubting the central mystery of the Catholic priesthood: the sacrifice of the mass. 'Perhaps it was not the Lord's flesh and blood! I confessed this thought and prayed. But I could not rid myself of it.'[2] He decided to read once through the Bible, and soon became immersed in a fascinated study of its pages. The realization began to dawn upon him, 'We have been deceived.'[3]

The result was a strange one, but just possible in those confused times. He continued as a Catholic priest, but let his sympathy be known for 'Reformation teaching'. Applying himself more seriously to his work, he was a popular curate and built a reputation as an 'evangelical preacher'. Yet he came to see afterwards that there had been no heart-changing experience. The guarded approval he gave to Luther's teaching was no more than mental assent. Lutheranism attracted him, but he occupied a well-paid and pleasant post, and had no wish to make life difficult for himself. Had things continued on their normal course he would either have continued as a priest, or drifted through circumstances into the Lutheran camp to become the type of half-hearted parish minister who was to cause the Reformer such grief and disappointment.

Instead, something happened which shattered his comfortable world. The execution took place in his district of 'a God-fearing pious hero, Sicke Snyder by name, who was beheaded because he had renewed his baptism'.[4] Simons was horrified by the execution, impressed by the martyr's demeanour and most of all intrigued by the odd idea of 'rebaptism'. Searching the Bible again with this in mind, he could find no reference to the baptism of infants.

Consultation with his own bishop and advice sought from several Lutherans, including Martin Luther himself, only confused him. He maintained that they all acknowledged the absence of paedobaptism from Scripture and then all gave different reasons for practising it. The break between Reformers and Radicals had now taken place, and he often found baptism to be the subject of earnest debate within his parish.

Anabaptists in fact were spreading into Holland, and the worldly priest with Lutheran leanings was very worried. The moral lives and religious earnestness of those he met impressed him. Yet there was a streak of wildness about them that repelled him. A strong interest in unfulfilled prophecy led them into odd speculations. Dangerous murmurs about setting up the kingdom of God were common among them. Menno had in fact come across a revolutionary wing of the movement destined to scandalize Europe and embarrass saner Anabaptists for a century. The grim work of imprisoning, torturing, burning, garrotting and drowning, which Lutherans and Catholics so enthusiastically organized against the 'heretics', was having a natural enough effect. Some of the Radicals were talking of armed resistance. The death of sober leaders threw power into the hands of unbalanced men. Fiery apocalyptic dreams began to appeal to the persecuted people.

The fanatics of Münster

In 1533 the explosion came. The German city of Münster, near the Dutch border, had declared itself Lutheran, expelled its Catholic bishop and then become increasingly influenced by Anabaptists. They were so powerful there that the usual persecution was impossible. The city soon became a refuge for harassed heretics of all types, and the more militant of them flocked there to establish a base for their schemes. Lutherans and Catholics united in an army and, led by the deposed bishop, laid siege to the city. Large numbers of enthusiasts, a lack of sober leadership, imminent danger and a minority of revolutionaries:

here were all the ingredients for an outbreak of fanaticism. Jan Matthew, a Dutch baker, and Jan of Leiden, a tailor, both of them paranoid characters much given to colourful visions and grandiose proclamations, took control of the defenders. They announced the setting up of the New Jerusalem, soon to be rescued from its enemies by the return of Christ. Community of property was introduced, polygamy was permitted and severe laws were enacted and enforced. After two year's siege, the city fell. The leaders were tortured to death and their followers mercilessly punished. Greatly exaggerated accounts of the excesses of the past two years rapidly spread and were eagerly believed. To respectable people, Münster proved that all Anabaptists were red revolutionaries, insane fanatics and immoral libertines.

It was very nearly the death-blow to Anabaptism. A renewal of fierce persecution throughout Europe inevitably followed. What was more harmful, the Radicals had lost the image of respectability and consistent living which had so often won them grudging respect.

These events were only a few miles distant from the perplexed 'evangelical priest' Menno Simons. Even closer at hand, he saw some of his own parishioners infected by the enthusiasm. They took up arms in defiant sympathy with Münster's torment and were viciously put down. He deplored their violence, yet knew the extremity of persecution which had driven them to it. He disowned their fanaticism, yet saw among them a zealous pursuit of truth, abandonment of earthly comforts and an assurance of God's favour which he himself lacked. Everyone joined together in scandalized condemnation of them, yet he shrewdly suspected that what he always called 'the Münster teaching' was only the lunatic fringe of a movement which by and large held to evangelical truth and promoted godliness of life.

Simons was now in great mental distress, feeling increasingly drawn to a movement which would involve him in unpopularity at best, and martyrdom at worst. At last, on the final day of 1536, twelve years after entering the priesthood, he made the open break with his old religion, and threw in his lot with the Anabaptists. The visible sign of his decision was the acceptance of 'rebaptism' for himself, and it is interesting to see how he viewed it: 'I have been enlightened by the Lord, converted, have fled from Babylon and entered Jerusalem. Surrendering myself to the Lord with body and soul, I committed myself into His gracious hand.'[5] In other words, he saw baptism as a personal act of faith, a renunciation of a false form of religion, an embracing of the people of God and a taking up of the cross of discipleship.

Simons accepted baptism at the hands of Obbe Phillips, a leader who had disowned the more flamboyant and violent Anabaptism of the Low Countries and was seeking to encourage others to do the same – with such success that many already referred to themselves as Obberites. Their form of baptism was by pouring water upon the head.

The Mennonite Renewal
For most of the following year Menno lived quietly, studying the Bible and avoiding trouble. This was not to last long. A group of Obberites, scattered leaderless and discouraged, implored him to organize them and to become their pastor. This plunged him into further hesitation and heart-searching, but after months of reflection he gave in to their request. It was the beginning of years of ceaseless labour, constant journeys, ever-present danger and hair-raising adventure. Having once committed himself to the task, he gave every ounce of energy to it. Before long, the 'Obberites' were the 'Mennonites', and his organizing genius was binding together the scattered congregations in a unity they had never known before.

Menno realized that if his followers were to survive the Münster scandal, four things were necessary. There must be a complete turning from fanaticism and prophetic dreams. There must be a disowning of the use of force, even in self-defence. There must be a visible organization with a trained and qualified ministry. There must be an exercise of discipline within the congregations.

In a sense Menno Simons was simply restoring the principles of the banished 'Swiss Brethren'. It was high time. The Radicals were in serious disarray. Even those who had avoided the excesses of the Low Countries' variety were discovering that 'regenerate membership' is an ideal easier to define than to achieve. A very sympathetic observer nevertheless described their tendency to externalism and rigidity: 'They persuade themselves that as soon as they are received outwardly... into their own self-gathered assemblies, they are the holy people of God. Frivolous judgments, self-love and spiritual pride abound.'[6] Here is criticism with a familiar ring. The hard fact is that enthusiastic Christians who separate from a 'system' very quickly create a new institution of their own which may well be as far from demonstrating the mind of Christ as is the one they have left.

Menno's disciplined organization did not entirely deal with the problem. But it created an honoured and respected movement which still exists in the twentieth century. More than that, the Baptist churches which form one of the major world-wide movements of Christianity in our own day, trace with gratitude to the Mennonites many of the insights to which they have given their own expression. With his system of ministerial succession, interdependence of congregations, and exercise of church discipline, Menno Simons proved that belief in a 'spiritual church' can be expressed in practice, and that the replacing of 'sacraments' with 'divine ordinances' of communion and baptism, which reflect the believer's inward state, can offer a unifying and eloquent alternative to a state church sacramental system.

Throughout Simons' lifetime the lesson was ignored. His own life was in constant danger, and it is surprising that he managed to die a natural death at the age of sixty-five. His followers in Germany and the Netherlands were harassed and attacked by Lutherans and Catholics alike. Denmark offered them sanctuary and was thoroughly disapproved of for doing so. They had proved their case, but Europe was not yet ready to admit it.

Enter John Calvin
Europe, in fact, was giving its attention to another reformer who was to lead Protestantism as far to the left as Menno had led Radicalism back towards the right. The year that Menno Simons decided to be baptized, John Calvin published his *Institutes of the Christian Religion*. When Menno Simons gave in to the pleadings of the Dutch Anabaptists to be their leader, John Calvin was yielding to the pleadings of Farel to lead the reforms at Geneva.

John Calvin represented (and came to lead) second generation Protestantism. Only eight years old when Luther's theses thundered around Europe, he never knew as an adult an undivided Christendom. A choice between two systems was open to him from the beginning. After training for law and priesthood, he made the choice, in a typically calm and irrevocable manner. A 'sudden conversion' to which he gave no date, committed him body, mind and heart to the service of the omnipotent God.

The purpose of this chapter is not to review Calvin's vast theological system in general, but to follow the course he took when it had to be worked out in practical terms at the local church level. For

the shy, asthmatic scholar who gave Christian doctrine its most systematic expression was not permitted to follow a life of letters as he
wished. A Frenchman, he found himself called to hammer out the
implications of his teaching in the Franco-Swiss city of Geneva. He
did it to such an effect that generations of Christians have looked to
that city as their spiritual home.

When he arrived there in 1536 an enormous task faced him. He
found the place notoriously lax in morals, ruled by a city council
jealous of its powers and inhabited by a populace more eager to throw
off Romanism than to embrace anything else. He found some evangelical believers who wished to take reform further than Luther had
done, troubled by the claims of Anabaptists and eager to have fellowship with those pre-Reformation Protestants, the Waldensians. The
relationship of these factors to the church system which he evolved
has not always been realized. Though the movement he led became
the greatest religious revolutionary force in Europe, Calvin never
claimed to be an innovator. Just as his *Institutes* were shaped by the
Apostles' Creed and his doctrine of God by Augustine, so it must
surely be acknowledged that his system of church discipline owed
much to the Anabaptists. The Radical movement as a whole he dis-
liked and distrusted, but he saw the force of many of its criticisms of
Lutheran and Zwinglian state-dominated churches. He was groping
towards the ideal of a free church in a free state.

Calvin saw the weakness of the optimistic assumption that
preaching and sacraments produced a true church. He added the third
characteristic of a reformed church: the exercise of spiritual discipline.
In doing so, he was emulating the Anabaptists. In doing so he also
gained for himself the caricature which has persisted ever since: that
of the black-avized dictator who interfered with every life and killed
every pleasure. He did this because he grafted the discipline of a
'regenerate church' on to the constitution of a 'comprehensive church'.
Defining membership of the church as the total of those who gave
approval to a scriptural declaration of faith (not to those who claimed
a personal experience of conversion) he then sought to mould them
into a pure church.

The priority of grace
What of baptism? Calvin not only preserved paedobaptism, but made
it a powerful weapon in his appeal both to the Catholic and the Ana-

baptist. Dismissing Luther's colourful speculations about the unborn baby's spiritual capacity, and denouncing the Anabaptist emphasis on the personal subjective experience of Christ before baptism, he built all his case around the priority of grace. Rejecting the arguments of those who demanded only the baptism of believers, he wrote, 'The delusion which misleads them is that they would always have the *thing* to precede the *sign*.'[7] But what precedes either is the grace of God. It is to that grace that any sacrament should supremely bear witness, not to the subjective condition at the moment of the person who receives it.

Calvin defined a sacrament as 'an external sign by which the Lord seals on our consciences His promises of good-will towards us, in order to sustain the weakness of our faith, and we in turn testify our piety towards Him, both before Himself, and before angels as well as men'.[8]

'We in turn' is the crux. Just as in all of life, so in the sacraments, God takes the initiative in approaching us; we in return then respond to him. This, said Calvin, really turning the tables on the Anabaptists, is best symbolised by paedobaptism. It does not put the baptismal candidate in the wrong position, but puts God in the right position, as sovereign giver of grace.

In the whole of his baptismal argument the Reformer revealed that his eyes were wide open to the popular appeal of the Anabaptists. He understood their arguments, married the widow of one of their ministers, and set out not only to rebut their claims, but to win back their converts to his own church system. Though he referred to them as 'frenzied spirits' who raise 'great disturbance in the Church on account of paedobaptism'[9] and 'furious madmen' who 'cease not to assail this holy ordinance',[10] he paid them the compliment of closely arguing every one of their beliefs. In so doing, he unconsciously bore witness to the essentially Christian and evangelical nature of his opponents. The principles he contended against are very much the principles of a modern baptist (even a Calvinistic baptist!). Certainly they are not the principles of either lunatics or heretics, though in the sixteenth century they were regularly assumed to be both.

The Anabaptist argument reflected in Calvin's writings rested on the discontinuity of the old and new covenants, the need for an evangelical experience to precede an evangelical ordinance, and the essential spirituality of the church as consisting only of believers. Calvin maintained the opposite. First, the old and new covenants are alike in foundation, meaning and purpose: they differ only in the external ordinances of initiation – circumcision for the old covenant, baptism for the new.

Therefore, secondly, since circumcision was administered to infants, even though it is said to symbolise both repentance and faith, so baptism can also be administered in the same condition.

Thirdly, to insist that only those who give what is conceived to be convincing proof of spiritual life are to be members of the church is again to displace grace from its essential position. Scriptures like Romans 6:2-4 and Galatians 3:27-29 do not say, 'Die to sin, put on Christ, and then you may be baptized and regarded as a church member.' They say, 'God in grace has called you by his word expressed in baptism and church fellowship: now make these things real by dying to sin and putting on Christ.'

Very neatly Calvin turned against the Anabaptists their reluctance to say that those who die in infancy before they can choose or reject Christ, are eternally lost. But if they are not lost, they are saved. And did not the actions and words of Christ underline this when he received little children, blessed them and said, 'to such belongs the kingdom of God' (Mark 10:14)?

Pressed as to what then was the condition of a baptized child, Calvin fell back once more on the priority of grace: 'God ... sanctifies whom He pleases.'[11] But how can that be? It 'is as possible and easy for Him as it is wondrous and incomprehensible for us'.[12] To the further objection that scripturally it is the hearing of the Word that leads to faith (Rom. 10:17), he replied that this is the usual, but not the invariable way:

> 'Those, therefore, whom the Lord is to illumine with the full brightness of His light, why may He not, if He so pleases, irradiate at present with some small beam ... I would not rashly affirm that they are endued with the same faith which we experience in ourselves, or have any knowledge at all resembling faith (this I would rather leave undecided); but I would somewhat curb the stolid arrogance of those men who, as with inflated cheeks, affirm or deny whatever suits them.'[13]

So the infants of Christian parents are to be baptized for future repentance and faith, while unbaptized adults who are capable of hearing and then believing or disbelieving, are required to display signs of repentance and faith before baptism, as were non-Jews under the old covenant when they approached circumcision.

What infant baptism achieves
What benefit does infant baptism then bring? To the parents it symbolises the grounds of hope which Christian parents have for their children, filling 'pious breasts with no ordinary joy, urging them more strongly to love their affectionate Parent, when they see that, on their account, He extends His care to their posterity ... seeing with the bodily eye the covenant of the Lord engraven on the bodies of their children'.[14] To the children it presents a powerful argument in later life for claiming the promises of God and embracing him in penitence and faith: 'Being ingrafted into the body of the Church, they are made an object of greater interest to the other members. Then when they have grown up, they are thereby strongly urged to an earnest desire of serving God.'[15]

The result of these efforts to placate, silence or win back the Radicals was in fact one of Calvin's least-known but most remarkable successes. In French Switzerland thousands of Anabaptists came into the field of Calvinism and had their children baptized. At the same time, agreement was reached between Calvinists and many of the Waldensians. These mysterious survivors of medieval 'heresy', practising baptism for both believers and their children, greeted with joy those who had left the doctrines of Rome and had accepted the Word of God. Their younger leaders were fascinated by Calvin's complete and logical system. The older leaders admired much of it, but held aloof from formal amalgamation. The two groups parted company, the younger bringing the Waldensians' wealth of experience into the Reformer's camp and experiencing in itself something akin to a religious revival.

Within a century Calvinism replaced Anabaptism as the most influential expression of Christianity in the Low Countries, became the persecuted but defiant Protestantism of France and Scotland, and the Christian orthodoxy of England and her colonies. In due course it would become the world-wide phenomenon of Reformed Christianity with consequences, at the beginning, unimaginable.

Calvin's teaching altered the whole content of the baptismal controversy. In the Middle Ages, paedobaptism stood for Catholicism, and adult baptism for evangelical 'heresy'. During the Lutheran

Reformation, paedobaptism symbolized state Christianity, while adult baptism symbolized voluntary Christianity. Through Calvin's reforms, paedobaptism came to represent a predestinarian view of the gospel, while adult baptism accompanied a strong emphasis on human free-will. As we showed in Part One, many would claim that this has remained the basic baptismal issue ever since. Others would warmly deny this.

References

1. Menno Simon's autobiography. Quoted in E. H. Broadbent, *The Pilgrim Church* (Pickering & Inglis, 1935), p. 186.
2. *Ibid.*
3. *Ibid.,* p. 187.
4. *Ibid.,* p. 186.
5. *Ibid.,* p. 190.
6. *Ibid.,* p. 186.
7. John Calvin, *Institutes,* IV. xvi. 21.
8. *Ibid.,* IV. xiv. 1.
9. *Ibid.,* IV. xvi. 1.
10. *Ibid.,* IV. xvi. 10.
11. *Ibid.,* IV. xvi. 17.
12. *Ibid.,* IV. xvi. 18.
13. *Ibid.,* IV. xvi. 19.
14. *Ibid.,* IV. xvi. 9.
15. *Ibid.*

8

The Politician and the Pot-mender

The Puritan era in England was an age that made legends. Like most legends they tend to the caricature rather than the literal truth. The very word 'Puritan' conjures up in many minds a picture of tall-hatted, long-faced, psalm-singing spoilsports, full of cant and hypocrisy. To others, the Puritans are the most apostolic men the world has known since the apostles themselves.

There were giants on the earth in those days and their names were household words. Seraphic Thomas Watson drew crowds to his parish church weekly to hear thirty-point sermons. Stern-faced John Owen's sonorous phrases held Parliament spellbound and influenced the nation's affairs. Warm-hearted Richard Baxter set every family in Kidderminster praying.

John Brown defied a ruthless king to establish the right of humble folk to worship God as their consciences dictated. John Smyth's restless mind drove him from Anglican to Presbyterian to Independent to Anabaptist, and produced the first English statement of religious toleration. Stocky John Bunyan preached to village congregations what he 'smartingly did feel' and made his prison the birthplace of a religious classic. William Rogers' pulpit pleadings threw hundreds of Essex hearers into a paroxysm of tears. Thomas Hooker's market-day lectures sharply reduced the crime rate in Chelmsford. And over the whole scene strode the massive and enigmatic figure of Oliver Cromwell, forcing democracy on a Parliament that suspected it, forcing godliness on a nation that rejected it, and forcing tolerance on a religion that denounced it.

Equally gigantic was the royal family of Stuart: four successive kings with a remarkable aptitude for choosing the wrong side. It cost one of them his head and another his throne. It hounded evangelicals to death or exile, and twice drove them in desperation to revolution.

Not surprisingly this was an age of intolerance. Mutual tolerance is one of the very few features of twentieth-century Christianity in which it can claim to be an improvement on the seventeenth century.

On the other hand, the people of the Puritan era took their souls and their God very seriously indeed: an attitude which twentieth-century man finds distinctly puzzling.

Two men stood out as particularly glowing examples of intense conviction combined with broad tolerance. They looked at baptism, as well as at other points of controversy, and got very close to a solution. Their names were John Owen and John Bunyan. To understand their contribution to the debate we must take a rapid look at the circumstances of their time.

The Church of England was the religion of the realm, by law established. The Church occupied a position definitely Protestant in doctrine, but in many ways Catholic in structure and practice. Every citizen was legally required to be baptized as an infant, to be confirmed as an adult and to attend public worship at an Anglican church. It was a perfect example of the 'sacralist society'.

Within the ranks of Anglicanism were growing numbers of 'Puritans' who wished to retain a state church, but were dissatisfied with its current condition, and bent on transforming it from within. Looking to Calvin's Geneva as their ideal, they aimed for a Calvinistic system of doctrine and a Presbyterian system of church government.

Outside the Church's ranks were the Dissenters or Separatists. They (on the whole) accepted Geneva's doctrine, but believed that it contradicted Geneva's practice. To them a pure and scriptural church must of necessity have a regenerate membership, and this meant the end of a state church. They gathered groups of Christians on the basis of personal confession of faith, and regarded them and their children alone as members of the true church. They became Independents or Congregationalists of later denominational life. In turn, some of them took the logic further: 'Surely,' they said, 'regenerate membership leads to baptism of believers only, and the rebaptism of those merely christened as infants.' Some were influenced by Dutch Mennonites and, discarding their Calvinistic theology, became 'General Baptists'. Others (the majority) preserved the theology of Geneva and became 'Particular Baptists'. The wheel had turned full circle. Calvinism had led to Anabaptism.

John Owen
Steering a dangerous course throughout this era and among these divided Christians was the universally respected figure of John Owen,

'the Calvin of England'. Converted at Oxford University, from the beginning he gave his immense mind to the statement and defence of Reformation doctrine. Manoeuvred out of college by High-Church enemies, he worked quietly as a chaplain until the outbreak of the Civil War, and then became rector of two successive Essex villages. At Fordham he was a Presbyterian, working hopefully within the established church. By the time he reached Coggleshall in 1646, he had come to Independent convictions, and wished to pastor a separated group of convinced Christians.

Nevertheless, at Coggleshall he pioneered a remarkable idea for combining a state system and a voluntary system of church government. He suggested an arrangement whereby ministers could fulfil a double function as 'rector' of a typically mixed parish and 'pastor' of groups within the parish of those who professed conversion and met as 'gathered churches'.

The scheme never really got off the ground outside Essex, but it showed how Owen's mind was working: he wished to see division among Christians reduced to an absolute minimum. As his influence grew and he became preacher to Parliament, chaplain to Cromwell, and Vice-Chancellor of Oxford University, he nursed his dream of evangelical unity. The Christians he met everywhere were essentially one in belief. They all bore the three classic marks of a true church: preaching of the truth, administration of the sacraments and exercise of discipline.

'Nor shall any man be able to prove but that, on the doctrinal agreement which we all profess, we may, notwithstanding the differences that remain, enjoy all that peace and union which are prescribed into the churches and disciples of Christ.'[1] In this he quite clearly included 'moderate' Anglicans, Presbyterians, Congregationalists and Baptists. His very affection for John Bunyan makes this clear, and many of his other actions underline the fact. This was in striking contrast to some of his colleagues, who regarded Baptists with unconcealed dislike, and labelled them 'Anabaptists' with all the unpleasant connotations of that word.

Saintly Thomas Watson, for example, a staunch Presbyterian whose ministry at St. Stephen's, Walbrook, was deeply effective in the heart of London, dropped all of his customary good sense and biblical argument when preaching on baptism: 'The baptism of persons grown up to maturity we may argue against from the ill consequences of it.

They dip the persons they baptize over head and ears in cold water and naked, which is as indecent as it is dangerous.'[2] Thus, he solemnly concluded, by being baptized naked (which of course they were not), the candidates encouraged immoral thoughts and thus broke the seventh commandment, while by encouraging them to do so, their ministers made them liable to catch cold and die, thus breaking the sixth commandment. Those who do these things are people of 'vile opinions and vicious practices', while their unbaptized children are 'sucking pagans'.[3] With debate at that kind of level, it is not surprising that any friendly spirit, let alone reconciliation, seemed impossible.

Yet in such a context, John Owen, probably the most widely read and influential of the Puritan theologians, was advocating the closest possible co-operation and the avoidance of hostility and distrust. He went further, and proposed intercommunion: the mutual acceptance of Christians at one another's celebration of the Lord's Supper:

> 'Where any ... make confession of that truth whereby they may abide in Christ and are preserved from pernicious seductions, although they may differ from us and the truth in some things of less moment, we are obliged not only to forbearance of them, but communion with them. For who shall refuse those whom Christ hath received? This and no other is the rule of our evangelical love and communion among ourselves. Whatever we require more ... is an unwarrantable imposition on their consciences or practice.'[4]

In 1654 Oliver Cromwell became Protector of the Commonwealth and head of state in an England which five years earlier had executed its king. One of the first results was his own remarkable attempt to achieve a just solution of the religious problems. He created what must surely be the most elastic state church ever conceived. Supported by public taxes, its clergy were appointed by 'Triers' responsible to Parliament. The only qualifications required of a minister were evangelical soundness of doctrine and evidence of a consistent character. Within those limits, he could be a Presbyterian, an Independent, or a Baptist and could lead his congregation in any of these paths. Prominent on the Board of Commissioners in charge of the whole complex scheme was John Owen. He must have been very happy indeed to serve in that capacity, for the scheme embodied principles which he had repeatedly advocated, and his influence is undoubtedly apparent in many of its details.

John Bunyan

In the town of Bedford, a little group of hitherto despised Christians was quick to grasp a dazzling opportunity. About two dozen were gathered together as a 'Gospel Church'. Under the leadership of John Gifford, an ex-Royalist Army Officer turned disreputable doctor and then dramatically converted, they had met quietly as a separatist church through all the recent troubled years 'without any form and order as to visible church communion ... zealous to edify themselves and to propagate the Gospel ... showing their detestation of the bishops and their superstitions.'[5] Were they Independent (Congregationalist) or Baptist? The two denominations, in a friendly way, have both claimed the allegiance of the group ever since and of the humble tinker who was to become its most illustrious member.

> 'The principle upon which they thus entered into fellowship one with another and upon which they did afterwards receive those that were added ... was faith in Christ and holiness of life, without respect to this or that circumstance or opinion in outward and circumstantial things.'[6]

So reads their own earliest account. They seem to have regarded the issue of baptism as an 'outward and circumstantial thing'. Conscience and Scripture apparently led them to hold believers' baptism by immersion as the ideal, and a little inlet of the River Ouse 'beneath an elm tree near the corner of Duck Mill Lane'[7] was their baptistery. However, they did not demand the ideal. Christians already baptized as infants in the established church could be received into membership of this group, and members who wished to have their children baptized seem to have been free to take them to the parish church for that purpose. Such an attitude was extraordinary at that time when Anglicans despised and oppressed Dissenters, when Independents regarded Anglicans as members of Antichrist, and Baptists demanded rebaptism and a complete disowning of every other denominational affiliation.

Suddenly this little group found itself respectable. The Rector of St. John's, Bedford, was ejected. Dissenter John Gifford passed the scrutiny of the Triers with flying colours, and found himself established as the new rector, with full permission to use the parish church for his flock and his faith. The same year there called at the rectory a troubled tinker named John Bunyan. For at least three years this rough labourer in his mid-twenties had been undergoing agonies of spiritual conflict. Possessed of a remarkable imagination, he clothed his thoughts with such vivid imagery that he heard and saw them as voices and visions. His spiritual pilgrimage was long, driving him to the verge of mental breakdown, before he found inner peace under Gifford's ministry. He was baptized under the elm tree and registered as number twenty-six on the church membership roll.

Before long John Bunyan was a famous preacher. Before long, too, Cromwell was dead, Charles II was on the throne and a cavalier Parliament was bent on revenge against the Puritans. In 1660 John Owen was expelled from Oxford and formed an Independent church in London. John Bunyan was to receive rougher treatment: twelve years in prison as an illegal preacher. From his prison cell his books began to pour. The imagination which had once hounded his conscience now flowered into an astonishing ability to write books which lit up the Bible and searched the heart to its depths.

Meanwhile, the Great Ejection in 1662 hurled two thousand Puritan ministers of the Church of England into expulsion, homelessness and harassment. At the same time, it ensured the survival of religious dissent in England. At one blow, the small and despised congregations of Independents and Baptists were joined by many of the most spiritual and intellectual of the Anglican clergy in a common nonconformist exile, while thousands of the most influential and educated members followed their ejected ministers. By 1672 the King had accepted the impossibility of crushing dissent even with the most savage legislation. For a mixture of reasons he insisted on a Declaration of Indulgence which permitted limited freedom. John Bunyan promptly applied for a licence to preach. The Bedford Meeting which had survived ten years of underground activity invited him to be their pastor, and permission was granted.

The new pastor had enjoyed plenty of time in prison to ponder on the real essentials of Christianity. He had a moving last letter from dying John Gifford to his beloved church to ponder too: 'Concerning separation from the Church about baptism, laying on of hands, anointing with oils, psalms or any externals, I charge every one of you as you will give account of it to our Lord Jesus Christ ... that none of you be found guilty of this great evil.'[8]

Dissent among the Dissenters!

Bunyan continued to accept this striking definition of baptism as an 'external' and its relegation to the ranks of varying local practices prevalent among dissenting churches. It was the key to his own church discipline and to the relationship of his church with other Christian bodies. It led him into a good deal of criticism. That same year his infant son was baptized at the parish church, presumably at the wish of his wife who never became a member of the Bedford Meeting. John was rapidly becoming a nationally known figure, and was generally regarded as a Baptist. His stricter Baptist colleagues became thoroughly alarmed at his 'compromising' attitude both in family and church life and a book appeared on the subject. Written by two well-known Baptist ministers, Paul and Kiffin, it was called *Some Serious Reflections on that Part of Mr. Bunyan's Confession of Faith Touching Church Communion with Unbaptized Persons.*

The *Confession* referred to, built its scheme of fellowship on the words of Romans 15:7, 'Welcome one another, therefore, as Christ has welcomed you.' It was too simplified an approach for enthusiastic Baptists, and they roundly castigated Bunyan in the abusive language normally employed in seventeenth-century religious debate. A swift reaction came from John's pen, called *Differences in Judgment on Water Baptism No Bar to Communion*. He replied trenchantly to their criticism and sounded a ringing call to love and tolerance. He applied on two principles: only God's people make up a local church, but all of God's people should be included.

What then of baptism? John was explicit: 'Touching showish or figurative ordinances ... I believe that Christ hath ordained but two in His Church, viz Water Baptism and the Supper of the Lord. But I count them not as fundamentals of our Christianity. Servants they are ... to teach and instruct us in the weighty matters ... It is possible to commit idolatry, even with God's own appointments.'[9] But can the Christian act of initiation really be considered 'not a fundamental'? He went on to a robust denial that baptism is in fact initiation. It is not the new covenant equivalent of circumcision. From Romans 2:28-29 and Philippians 3:1-4 he argued that the new covenant 'circumcision' is a renewed heart and a right spirit. 'He is not a real Jew who is one outwardly, nor is true circumcision something external and physical. He is a Jew who is one inwardly, and real circumcision is a matter of the heart, spiritual and not literal. His praise is not from men but from God.' 'We are the true circumcision, who worship God in spirit, and glory in Christ Jesus, and put no confidence in the flesh.'

So initiation is not baptism, but the inward change of heart which begins the Christian life. Baptism is merely the outward sign of that inward change, and whether and how to be baptized are personal acts of obedience. To regard baptism as a church sacrament is to lift the baptismal controversy into an area where it is bound to confuse and divide. In that case, 'If Water Baptism ... trouble their peace, wound the consciences of the godly, dismember and break their fellowship: it is, although an ordinance, for the present *to be prudently shunned* ... for the edification of the Church is to be preferred before it.'[10]

This was strong stuff, and of course it opened the Bedford pastor to the charge that he was trying to resolve the baptismal problem, not with a baptismal theology, but with a non-theology. *How Long is it Since You Were a Baptist?* asked the next pamphlet to be issued, and in his further reply, entitled *Peaceable Principles and True*, Bunyan gave the spirited reply that he was happy to leave the title 'Baptist' with the only man to whom the Bible gives it – John the Baptist. As far as John Bunyan was concerned:

> 'Since you would know by what name I would be distinguished from others; I tell you, I would be and hope I am a Christian. As for these factious titles of Anabaptists, Independents, Presbyterians or the like, I conclude that they came neither from Jerusalem nor Antioch, but rather from Hell and Babylon, for they naturally tend to divisions.'[11]

John Owen was well aware of these opinions. He had long admired his less academic but more eloquent fellow-minister, and had used his influence in court and church circles to hasten Bunyan's release from prison. The tinker had shown his *Pilgrim's Progress* to the statesman, who was so impressed that he sent it on to his own publisher. He also intended to write an Introduction to Bunyan's defence of his baptismal practice but was dissuaded by other Baptists. The universal church is the loser. Owen on Baptism is a treasure we can ill afford to be without. Bunyan accepted the disappointment philosophically. 'Perhaps it is more for the glory of God that truth should go naked into the world, than as seconded by so mighty an armour-bearer as he.'[12]

In any case, events were pressing Christians into a unity of sympathy and purpose greater than any denominational division. James II succeeded his brother Charles to the throne, and a king with a secret sympathy for the papacy was replaced by a king who openly espoused Roman Catholicism. The Church of England found itself as harassed as the dissenters. The Archbishop of Canterbury and six bishops were imprisoned and on trial. Dissenting ministers visited them in prison and knelt in prayer with their arms around them. A common Protestantism was now at stake, and divided Christians closed ranks. Included in the movement towards closer evangelical fellowship were both Calvinist and Arminian Baptists, threatened by persecution without and false doctrine within. They began to see (and to admit) that a paedobaptist who is orthodox is more to be welcomed than a Baptist who is heretical. To such a proposition many evangelical baptists in the twentieth century would give hearty assent.

By 1688, many in the country, sickened by a century of conflict, said, 'Away with these Stuarts and their religion: we want a Protestant nation and freedom of conscience.' By then, too, Christians had learnt their need of each other. If they could not reconcile their differences, they could hold them in love and mutual respect. For Nonconformists (with the exception of the Strict Baptist Movement) the intercommunion for which John Owen had contended became increasingly common. More and more Christians gave their approval to John Bunyan's declaration: 'I will not let water baptism be the rule, the door, the bolt, the bar, the wall of division between the righteous and the righteous.'[13]

References

1. William Goold (ed.), John Owen, *Collected Works* (Banner of Truth, 1965-66), Vol. 15, p. 220. For biographical details of the life of Owen, see biography by Andrew Thomson (Christian Focus, 1996).
2. Thomas Watson, *The Ten Commandments* (Banner of Truth, 1962), p. 221.
3. *Ibid.*, p. 163.
4. Goold, *op. cit.*, Vol. 4, p. 147. Italics ours.
5. *The Bunyan Meeting Book.* Quoted in Brittain, *In the Steps of John Bunyan* (Rich & Cowan, 1950), p. 145.
6. *Ibid.*, p. 146.
7. *Ibid.*, p. 149.
8. *Ibid.*, p. 157.
9. George Offor (ed.), *The Works of John Bunyan* (Blackie & Son, 1848), Vol. 2, p. 604.
10. *Ibid.*, Vol. 2, p. 609.
11. *Ibid.*, Vol. 2, p. 649.
12. *Ibid.*
13. *Ibid.*, Vol. 2, p. 656.

9

Revival and Expansion

The end of the Puritan era drew a line under the baptismal controversy. Not, of course, that the controversy was settled, but the issues having been raised, the lines of division were thereafter drawn in an increasingly permanent way. Christians became either infant or adult baptists, mutually exclusive and hence ignorant, suspicious and intolerant of each other's practice and belief. From time to time, movements of religious revival raised again the problems associated with different baptismal positions, and sometimes possible solutions to the controversy were proposed. Not, however, until the twentieth century did baptism become, once more, a subject of major importance to the whole of the Christian church.

Methodism and the Evangelical Awakening
The Evangelical Awakening in the eighteenth century was one of the most astonishing forward surges of the Christian church. Bringing new life and enthusiasm to the formal Christianity of England, Scotland, Wales and the American colonies, its influence was decisive at a time when the Anglo-Saxon peoples were beginning to shape the course of world history. The widespread Methodist movement was one result of a work of revival which swept tens of thousands of converts into the churches, deepened the life and witness of every denomination and purged Britain of many of the ills and injustices which had brought her to the brink of revolution.

At first sight, baptism does not seem to have been an issue in those exciting times. But a closer look reveals that every one of the great leaders of the revival had a hard tussle with the subject. The question which arose was not so much 'Who should be baptized?' but 'What does it accomplish?' For the double rediscovery that was made by the great evangelists was, first, the doctrine of justification by faith alone, and second, the possibility of a present subjective experience of pardon and assurance. The heart-experience of John Wesley, 'strangely warmed', was echoed in the life of every one of the leaders. George Whitefield in England, Howell Harris in Wales, William Tennant in America, Peter Böhler of Germany, all found the same great assurance, and preached it to thronging thousands:

> Thine eye diffused a quickening ray,
> – I woke, the dungeon flamed with light;
> My chains fell off, my heart was free,
> I rose, went forth, and followed Thee.[1]

So they sang, for so it had happened to each and every one.

This change was referred to in its scriptural terms of 'conversion', 'new birth' and 'regeneration'. It was the fundamental and distinctive doctrine of the whole great movement. But the very terms used raised a painful problem. Most of the leaders of first and second rank were faithful sons of the Church of England. Throughout their lives they struggled to remain within the Anglican fold and to keep their converts there. Their 'societies', which in the next generation became separate Methodist or Presbyterian churches, were at first simply groups of converts within the established church, forming an *ecclesiola in ecclesia*. Yet here came the difficulty. At the very heart of the service for Infant Baptism in the Book of Common Prayer which they acknowledged and used, were the words, 'Seeing now ... dearly beloved ... that this child is regenerate ...' If the great majority of their hearers had been regenerated in infancy through baptism, how could the evangelists press upon them their present need for regeneration through repentance and faith in Christ?

George Whitefield, who pioneered evangelistic preaching in churches and in the open air, well knew the danger of dependence on ecclesiastical ceremonies. Only a long struggle had freed him from it. 'God showed me that I must be born again, or be damned! I learnt that a man may go to church, say his prayers, receive the sacrament, and yet not be a Christian. How did my heart rise and shudder!'[2] '[But] oh what joy unspeakable filled my soul when the weight of sin went off, and an abiding sense of the pardoning love of God broke in upon my disconsolate soul!'[3]

In the first sermon preached after his ordination, Whitefield caused a sensation by pressing the need for an immediate conscious conversion to Christ. He expounded and distinguished the meanings of the phrase 'in Christ'. First, we can be said to be in Christ by outward profession through being baptized into Christ's church. But in fact with most people this has little consequence; church life is either ignored or formally observed. So those who have been 'born of water' in baptism must also be 'born of the Spirit' in conversion – or to employ John the Baptist's phrase in place of Christ's, those who have merely been 'baptized with water' need to be 'baptized with the Holy Ghost'.

This approach was adopted by many of the revival preachers, especially if, like Whitefield, their theology was Puritan and Calvinistic. They saw baptism in covenantal terms, were embarrassed by the use of the word 'regeneration' in connection with it and would have preferred its application to infancy to be limited to the children of godly parents.

> God seals to saints His glorious grace
> and not forbids their infant-race.
> Their seed is sprinkled with His blood,
> their children set apart for God,
> His Spirit on their offspring shed,
> like water poured upon the head.[4]

When such preachers mentioned baptism they usually had one of two purposes. Either it had a negative lesson: a warning that no external ceremony, however sacred, could change the human heart or remove the need for a personal encounter with Christ. Or it had a positive lesson: the memory of baptism stood as a visible and objective pledge from God that he who received and blessed an unconscious and undeserving infant is equally willing to receive and forgive the vilest outcast who cries to him for mercy.

The approach of the Wesley brothers was curiously different. They felt more bound by the *Book of Common Prayer* than most of their contemporaries and most of their converts. When touching upon baptism, John often used the dutiful phrase, 'our Church supposes' or 'it is the teaching of our Church'. Before his own conversion he firmly believed in 'baptismal regeneration' as he saw it taught in a church which, in the words of Lord Chatham, had Calvinistic Articles, Arminian ministers and a Romish liturgy.

After his conversion John Wesley saw that this would not do. His solution was completely original. At baptism, he suggested, infants are born again of the Holy Spirit and cleansed from inherited sin. But as a matter of observed fact, each then grows into a life of personal

sin and rejects the grace of God, thus forfeiting the eternal life granted
in baptism. Each then needs to be regenerated a second time by adult
conversion. We need, as it were, to be born again, again![5]

Charles Wesley embraced this idea, and expressed it quite clearly
in some of his hymns:

> When e'er the pure baptismal rite
> Is duly ministered below,
> The heavens are opened in our sight
> And God His Spirit doth bestow;
> The grace infused invisible
> Which would with man forever dwell.
>
> But oh, *we lost the grace bestowed,*
> Nor let the Spirit on us remain;
> Made void the ordinance of God,
> By sin *shut up the heavens again,*
> Who would not keep our garments white
> Or walk as children of the light.[6]

It made an effective instrument in evangelism. When John Wesley
cried to Anglican hearers, 'Lean no more on the staff of that broken
reed, that ye were born again in baptism,' his emphasis was on the
word *were*.[7] He did not mean that their baptism was ineffective *at the
time*; he meant that they had rendered it ineffective *since*.

At the same time, both of the Wesleys were quite busy baptizing
adults, as an outcome of their evangelistic journeys. They would never
rebaptize those already christened in infancy within the Church of
England. But they cheerfully dismissed the baptism of infants by
Nonconformists, and thus treated alike converts not baptized at all
and those baptized as infants in dissenting chapels. Many a riverbank
was the scene of enthusiastic baptismal services conducted by the
Wesleys. Some they baptized *because* they had experienced conversion. Others were baptized as anxious enquirers in *order* to be converted, and often as they emerged from the water, 'God filled their
hearts with peace and joy unspeakable in that very moment.'[8]

Nor surprisingly, the Baptists used these events to strengthen their
own case for the universal need of adult baptism. Numbers of Methodist societies became Baptist churches, and Charles Wesley, furious
with this 'carnal, cavilling, contentious sect, always watching to steal

away our children and make them as dead as themselves',[9] prevailed on his brother to write *A Treatise on Baptism - a Preservative against Unsettled Notions in Religion.* This leaflet defended the double practice of infant and adult baptism.

In England, it was all something of a side issue, but the story was very different in the American colonies. Here Methodism in turn gave birth to a huge expansion of Baptist growth. Both movements enjoyed popular appeal with the frontier mentality which valued self-government, suspected hierarchies in every form and yearned for emancipation from the past. But, between the two, Baptists had the advantage, for Methodists still wore some of the 'clinging rags' of Anglicanism and clericalism!

Adult baptism, often administered by lay folk with cheerful disregard for liturgy or form, echoed exactly the revival experience of sudden and deeply felt conversion. At the same time, most Baptists swung increasingly towards an Arminian expression of the gospel, thus lining up with Methodists and abandoning the (equally revived) Presbyterians and Congregationalists.

In the home country, development was quite different. Wesleyan Methodists were generally unimpressed by the Wesleys' own baptismal theories. Once they separated from the Church of England (after John's death, for it could never have happened during his life) they adopted a somewhat equivocal approach to the rite.

The Prayer Book words, 'this child is regenerate', were quietly dropped and replaced by a non-committal formula and a wide diffusion of practice. By the next century this led to the oft-repeated saying that, for Methodists, baptism means whatever the current local minister wants it to mean!

Understandably irritated, present-day Methodist leadership has become rather sensitive. Ministers now are expected to play it carefully by the book. Occasional attempts by the more evangelically minded to let 'rebaptism' in by the back door receive short shrift.

The modern *Methodist Service Book* suggests three different appropriate points for baptism: (1) shortly after birth (for children with Christian parents); (2) during older childhood or adolescence (after careful instruction); (3) in adult years (it is assumed, after conversion and instruction). For infants, the moving phrase is used: 'We claim for him/her all that Christ has won for us.'

A prelude to the Methodist rite avers, 'from our side baptism requires a response of repentance and faith in Christ as Lord and Saviour'. (How, one might wonder, can this imply anything other than the baptism of believers?) It may be administered to an infant, in anticipation of a response to be made later, or to a young person or an adult in recognition of a response already made to the grace of God.[10]

The ingenious wording of the whole service holds together in creative tension the three historic strands of Methodism: its roots in high church sacramentalism; its growth through evangelistic revival; and its experience of pragmatic personal and corporate discipline (that *Method* which earned its followers their distinctive name).

Conclusion

The story of the eighteenth-century revival on both sides of the Atlantic highlights the problem that baptismal belief repeatedly raises in times of evangelistic endeavour and spiritual fervour. The consequences are still with us.

Within the Church of England, Whitefield's Calvinistic evangelicalism was preserved and extended through the Evangelical Party. A century later this led to conflict with the emerging Anglo-Catholic Movement about baptismal regeneration. The Catholic wing maintained that the words, 'this child is regenerate', mean exactly what they say. Evangelicals replied that they must mean something else, since the Scriptures (and several of the Thirty-Nine Articles) clearly teach salvation by faith alone.

Indeed, a staple feature in evangelical Anglican preaching was the oft-repeated warning that sacraments alone cannot save. The message infuriated some (Charles Simeon was sometimes locked out of his pulpit by angry churchwardens for it), but enlightened and rescued many who went on to ask, then what *can* save me?

This still left a question unanswered: if sacraments cannot save me, what is their purpose? John Charles Ryle, first Church of England bishop of Liverpool, was an inveterate foe, as he saw them, of all things Roman, and a powerful advocate of the gospel of grace. He used to take each young ordinand for a walk in the episcopal garden in order to explain the true resolution of the baptismal conundrum – one of the 'Knots Untied' as he described it in his book of the same name. Unfortunately, many of the ordinands found the explanation so elaborate that they finished up with what was widely known as the 'baptismal headache'. The knot remained stubbornly tangled!

The story of revival and growth in the eighteenth and nineteenth centuries has brought us more than once into the twentieth century in which baptismal issues, complete with headaches, found startling and hitherto unsuspected new forms.

References

1. Charles Wesley, *The Methodist Hymn Book*, 1933, no. 371.
2. Arnold Dallimore, *George Whitefield* (Banner of Truth, 1970), p. 73.
3. *Ibid.,* p. 77.
4. George Whitefield. Quoted in Bernard G. Holland, *Baptism in Early Methodism* (Epworth, 1970), p. 122f.
5. See *ibid.,* ch. 6.
6. Quoted in *ibid.,* p. 67.
7. E. H. Sugden (ed.), *Wesley's Standard Sermons* (Epworth, 1921), Vol. 1, p. 296.
8. Nehemiah Curnock (ed.), *The Journal of the Rev. John Wesley* (1909), Vol. 6, p. 49, for one of many similar examples.
9. Thomas Jackson (ed.), *Wesleyan minister: Memoirs of the Rev. Charles Wesley* (1848), Vol. 2, p. 128.
10. Quotations from *The Methodist Service Book* (Methodist Publishing House, 1990).

10

Missionary Movements

Christians, inevitably, are missionary people. The Gospel writers all record Christ's final commission to his disciples in terms of commands to 'Go ...'[1] The Acts of the Apostles records the evangelistic expansion of Christian faith from Jerusalem to Rome. New Testament letters record how the gospel first reached the readers, and include advice and encouragement to pass on the faith to others. Central to the command was the obligation to baptize.[2] Ever since, the story of Christianity has been one of expansion and growth. As with an incoming tide, there have been times of withdrawal, suffering and retreat. But each has been followed by greater waves of successful missionary endeavour, creating an overall impression of steady growth over the long term. Today, estimates suggest that one person in three throughout the world owes allegiance in some form to Jesus Christ.

Because baptism is part of the process of expansion, periods of growth have shaped the practice of baptism and, in turn, have been shaped by it. In the early chapters of this book we showed how a suffering church in the second and third centuries developed the Catechumenate and invested the act of baptism for believing adults with moving ceremony and solemn vows. Later, from the fourth to the sixth centuries, when growth and expansion enjoyed State support and subsidy, the emphasis changed. Infant baptism became more usual, even normal, and the pre-baptismal Catechumenate was replaced by post-baptismal instruction in worship and discipleship.

From the thirteenth to the twentieth centuries Christian expansion has largely followed the growing worldwide political influence of European and Anglo-Saxon nations. Their Christians have taken the gospel with them, and of course, their Christianity and their baptismal practices have been coloured by their own cultural norms. At the end of the twentieth century Third World Christianity in all its new and exciting diverse forms is a new force worldwide. In turn, new forms of baptismal belief and practice will find expression in the century to come.

Roman Catholic missionary enterprise

Early European expansion was largely pioneered by courageous navigators, financed by the kings and queens of Spain and Portugal. In the fifteenth and sixteenth centuries they sailed west in search of the East, with its rich pickings of the spice trade. On the way they discovered the New World. Solidly loyal to the bishop of Rome, every crew included a priest. Unashamedly sacralist, when new lands were found, the discoverers claimed them, not only for the sovereign who had sent them, but for the Catholic Church as well.

These medieval Iberian and Italian Christians held crudely literalist *ex opere operato* views of baptism. To them, the act of baptism in itself effected salvation. Faith, of a sort, might follow later. After one harrowing transatlantic voyage, the surviving sailors were bemused, on reaching land, to find themselves hailed as gods by the local tribespeople. Dusky girls were more than accommodating, and the sailors – well, the sailors were sailors. In the end, even the priest protested at their promiscuity, complaining at the way they were satisfying themselves with so many heathen women. 'Oh, we're not,' the sailors replied, 'we baptize them first!'

Later, the *conquistadores* of central and southern America, again, always accompanied by priests, had no qualms in baptizing whole villages by spraying them wholesale with holy water in the name of the Father, the Son and the Holy Spirit. An entire Christian community created in a few moments! Christian instruction then followed, by gentle persuasion if possible, but by force if necessary. Thus, after a fashion, Latin America was won for Christ; or was it? Protestant Christians would later complain bitterly at the bewildering mixture of Roman ritual and pagan superstition which came to characterize much of the Christianity of the Continent. When they tried to bring what they considered to be the light of the gospel to those they regarded as still living in heathen darkness they were persecuted without mercy, not only by the local priests, but by the police who were always at their beck and call.

It would be tempting, as a consequence, to dismiss Roman Catholic missionary enterprise as nothing more than the inculcation of formal religion, which, far from drawing people to Christ, actually puts obstacles in their path. Much of the 'Christianization' of Latin America was undoubtedly flawed, and many modern Catholics will admit this. But there is another side to the story. Latin American Catholicism has its own impressive array of saints and martyrs. In the twentieth century it has given liberation theology to the world, with its biblical concern for the poor and for freedom from political tyranny.

Nor should pioneering work by Ignatius Loyola (c. 1491-1556) be forgotten. His founding of the Society of Jesus (the Jesuits) was originally a call to the priority of world mission. Culturally sensitive evangelism was developed in India and the Far East in the sixteenth century under the leadership of the first Jesuit missionary, Francis Xavier, and his successors. It followed in Mexico and the south-western United States and among tribespeople in Paraguay and Brazil in the seventeenth century. A century before David Livingstone pioneered the gospel in southern and central Africa, there was a short-lived Christian Kingdom of Kongo, with its own African bishops who visited Rome to petition for the abolition of slavery.

Jesuits ensured that Roman Catholicism would become and remain a worldwide force. Understandably reviled for centuries among Protestants, against whom they campaigned with relentless zeal, their contribution to world mission is nevertheless now recognized. Like all Catholics, however, the Jesuits baptized first (both adult converts and their children) and taught afterwards. Ignatius himself is reputed to have originated the somewhat ambiguous maxim, 'Give me a child till the age of six and you may do what you like with it afterwards.'

Protestants and evangelicals

The Evangelical Awakening of the eighteenth century led in turn to a great period of expansion for Protestant and evangelical Christianity throughout the world in the nineteenth century. Though it coincided with, and owed something to, the parallel expansion of European culture and 'colonialism', it was certainly not its automatic accompaniment. Indeed, much European Christianity was purely nominal except when touched by times of revival. Very many Europeans discarded it when they emigrated. Much of the spirit of their colonial expansion was flatly contrary to the spirit of the gospel, and made evangelism more difficult. 'The spread of Christianity in connexion with the expansion of Europe was chiefly through minorities, sometimes small minorities, who committing themselves fully to it, became expressions of the abounding vitality inherent in the Gospel.'[3]

Regrettably, this forward movement carried the denominational differences of Europe (and particularly Britain) with it. Easy to criticize now, it is difficult to see how it could have been avoided at the time. Conversions eventually came in a flood, but only after long periods when the missionaries laboured on alone and unencouraged. William Carey, the pioneer of them all, had to wait seven years for his first convert in India. Missionaries on the west coast of Africa, with an average life expectancy there of eighteen months, sometimes died without seeing one result. Naturally enough, they practised Christianity in the way they were used to it. A particular cultural expression of the Faith provided a link with home in a hostile land.

Baptists were first in the field, with the Baptist Missionary Society opening up India in 1792 and then the Congo basin in Africa. Congregationalists of the London Missionary Society reached the South Pacific in 1795, and Presbyterians of the Scottish Missionary Society made Africa their target a year later. Anglicans of the Church Missionary Society were in Africa by the last year of the century, and seventeen years later the Wesleyan Methodist Missionary Society had reached the West Indies. By 1815 American Protestantism was also reaching out with a zeal and vision which would ultimately enable the Americans to replace the British as the major source of funds and personnel for world Protestant evangelism.

Naturally, all the missionary societies practised adult baptism because they all made adult converts. In this they resembled the New Testament apostles. Yet even in the first generation the old divisions reappeared, for all except baptists were willing to baptize adult converts and their children. Indeed, when mass movements emerged, Anglicans and Presbyterians were willing to baptize whole villages or areas. The result was that areas of the world adopted forms of Christianity in which baptismal practices depended on the denominational source from which the pioneer missionaries came. The 'average' Christian in Zaire today, for example, is very likely to have been baptized as an adult believer. His counterpart in East Africa will most likely have received infant baptism.

A second missionary era began when evangelical Christianity was in decline in the established denominations in Europe and America. Suspecting the liberal or sacramental tendencies which were rapidly gaining ground, a new generation of missionaries established the great 'faith missions'. These were organized outside denominational leadership, and drew support from evangelicals across the whole spectrum of Protestantism. So, for example, Hudson Taylor's work led to the foundation of the China Inland Mission, now the Overseas Missionary Fellowship; C. T. Studd's to the forming of the Worldwide Evangelization Crusade, and indirectly to the starting of the Unevangelized Fields Mission. Many societies like them possessed no denominational pattern to import to the 'mission-field'. They concentrated on building indigenous churches and handing them the Scriptures as quickly as possible. As a matter of recorded fact, they usually established adult baptism as normal, and the vast indigenous and independent movements that now inherit their work largely continue that policy.

The Brethren movement

The Brethren movement began in the 1830s, as an expression of desire for true spiritual unity in Christ. Early leaders like J. N. Darby and George Müller believed that the biblical concept of the church as the Body of Christ was confused and denied by the existence of separate organised denominations and a separate class of clergy. Their desire for Christians to worship together solely on the basis of their fellowship with Christ, struck a chord in many hearts. Without any visible organization or appointed leadership, the idea spread rapidly.

However, from the beginning there were differences of approach which made eventual division inevitable. Some, like Müller, who became known as 'Open Brethren', saw their duty as a recovery of New Testament principles and practice. As they clarified their beliefs they came to the baptist position, establishing independent assemblies of believers practising only believers' baptism. Their distinctive opposition to ordained clergy kept them separate from Baptists in Britain and America and wherever their missionaries did their immensely fruitful work on every continent. Movements closely akin to them emerged: the 'Little Flock' of China and the Bakht Singh movement of India. In Germany and Russia, under pressure from hostile governments, they found their views on baptism sufficiently close to enter into union with Baptists and Pentecostals in the twentieth century.

Darby's approach to rebuilding the New Testament church was very different. This ex-clergyman from the Church of England was one of those few original and idiosyncratic thinkers that each generation throws up. Posing the question, 'Are Christians competent to form organised churches after the model of the primitive churches?'

he replied, 'No! For the Church is in a state of ruin ... The first departure is fatal ... the Scripture never recognises a recovery from such a
state.'[4] What then should conscientious Christians do? 'They ought
to meet in the unity of the Body of Christ outside the world, taking
heed of the promise of Christ that where two or three gather together
in His Name, He is present.'[5] One curious result of this approach was
that the Exclusive Brethren (who accepted Darby's view) adopted
from the beginning an approach to baptism which had the potential to
resolve many of the difficulties between paedobaptists and baptists.

Baptism, Darbyites suggested, is always and only connected with
visible profession and admission to external privilege. It brings the
baptized, not into the enjoyment of forgiveness, regeneration, and so
on, but into the circle of Christian profession where these things are
taught and sought. 'Believers' baptism', they asserted, is no more a
literal biblical expression than 'infant baptism'. An adult person is
properly baptized for the remission of sins, to put on Christ, and is
buried with Christ by baptism (Acts 2:38; Gal. 3:27; Rom. 6:4). 'The
really important moment as to baptism for us as believers is when we
realise what is involved in it, and accept in our souls that to which we
were committed in baptism. We are baptized not because we are saved
but because we are lost.'[6] This convoluted syntax and inverted logic
typifies the kind of argument pioneered by Darby and earnestly imitated by his disciples in every area of church life. In similar fashion
he argued that at Communion we celebrate the *absence* of Christ,
because, in the apostle's words, we do it, 'until he comes'.

As far as the baptism of infants was concerned, Exclusive Brethren maintained the principle of 'household baptism' and accepted
wholeheartedly the classic reformed arguments for it. If Jesus is Lord
to a new convert, then 'Jesus is Lord to all his household, whose
members are thus introduced to the outward circle of profession and
privilege of Christianity'.[7] Though this approach implies only the
baptism of believers and their children, Exclusive Brethren generally
recognize indiscriminate infant baptism as an existential fact often
prevailing outside their own ranks, and neither demand nor favour
rebaptism. On the other hand, if a convert already baptized in infancy
feels troubled in conscience and asks for adult baptism, this is normally made possible.

Because of other developments within their ranks, the teachers of
these views are scarcely known or listened to by other Christians.

This is a pity, for the fact is that they have found a successful way of combining the regular practice of infant baptism and believers' baptism within an evangelistic framework, and with room for freedom of conscience in the sticky matter of rebaptism.

Baptists and Tractarians

While the Exclusive Brethren were finding their own solution to the baptismal controversy, opinion in the older churches continued to harden. In June 1864 Charles Haddon Spurgeon, perhaps the most outstanding Nonconformist minister of the whole nineteenth century, preached a celebrated sermon on the subject of baptismal regeneration. His target was not so much the practice of paedobaptism *per se*, it was rather the position then being asserted by the leaders of the Tractarian Movement in the Church of England that salvation was effected only through baptism. Spurgeon's language was uncompromizing: 'Out of any system which teaches salvation by baptism must spring infidelity ... which the false Church already seems willing to nourish and foster beneath her wing. God save this favoured land from the brood of her own established religion!'[8] However, on the same basis Spurgeon attacked the Evangelical wing of the Church of England, and withdrew from the Evangelical Alliance because of their membership within it.

Not surprisingly, Spurgeon's language was repaid in kind as a stream of tracts and counter-tracts appeared, similar in the bitterness of their language to earlier conflicts between Reformers and Anabaptists. By the end of the century, Anglo-Saxon Christians were either firmly baptist or adamantly paedobaptist – and knew the reasons why. So great was the mutual hostility between them that it was unthinkable for an adult baptized in infancy to consider rebaptism as a believer, while Baptists could be expelled from their churches even for attending an infant baptismal service! Meanwhile pan-denominational movements like the Keswick Convention and the Evangelical Alliance pursued a policy of letting sleeping dogs lie. The subject of baptism was a 'secondary issue', on which we should agree to differ – and agree to keep quiet too!

Yet, for all this controversy, to many Christians in Europe at the end of the nineteenth century, the end of the church's mission was clearly within sight:

Nearer and nearer draws the time,
the time that shall surely be.
When the earth shall be filled with the glory of God
as the waters cover the sea.[8]

How wrong they were! How the turmoil and change of the twentieth century would destroy their triumphalist optimism! And how the decline of Christianity in the West and its unprecedented expansion in the Third World would end the rancour of baptismal controversy, drawing Christians together in humble re-examination of their beliefs, and in working together, despite their differences, for the glory of God and his kingdom!

References

1. See, e.g. Matthew 28:19,20; Mark 16:15; Luke 24:47; John 20:21; Acts 1:8
2. See Matthew 28:19
3. K. S. Latourette, *A History of Christianity* (Eyre & Spottiswoode, 1954), p. 924.
4. E. H. Broadbent, *The Pilgrim Church* (Pickering & Inglis, 1935), p. 374f.
5. *Ibid.,* p. 377.
6. *Letters of C. A. Coates* (Stow Hill Bible and Tract Depot), p. 33.
7. *Ibid.*
8. C. H. Spurgeon, Metropolitan Tabernacle Pulpit, 1864, p. 328.
9. A. C. Ainger's hymn, *God is working his purpose out,* still included in many hymn books.

11

Mission, Unity and Renewal

Massive and unprecedented change has marked the twentieth century. Christianity in all its strands has been affected as much as any other group and society. Two world wars, the rise and demise of atheistic Communism, the end of European colonialism, the resurgence of Islam and the secularizing of what was once the heart of Christendom; developments like these have forced the leaders and members of all Christian churches to examine their meaning and purpose.

This has brought both threat and opportunity. On the one hand, the old Christianity of Europe has slipped into what seems at times to be terminal decline. On the other hand, the collapse of colonialism, though confidently expected to signal the end of the 'white man's religion', has actually coincided with an astonishing expansion of the church in Africa and Asia. Where Livingstone and Carey numbered converts of a lifetime in single figures, they are now reckoned in tens of millions. In South America, established Catholic religion is now challenged by vibrant Pentecostalism. In the United States, in contrast to other highly technological societies, pervasive folk-religion has turned the phrase 'born again' into a contemporary slogan. Asian societies like those of South Korea and the Philippines have become Protestant and Catholic cultures respectively. As the newly Christianized sub-continents inherit the vision of mission, roles are oddly reversed.

Amidst these whirling tides of change and turmoil three significant movements have profoundly affected baptismal belief and practice. They are the expansion of world mission, the growth of ecumenism, and the spread of charismatic renewal.

The expansion of world mission
All the historic churches of Western Europe have suffered dramatic numerical decline during the twentieth century. This has forced them all to reconsider mission, its theology and practice. With this has come re-examination of baptismal belief and expression.

The link between evangelism and baptism is obvious. Baptism has to do with initiation, the way people become Christians and members of the church. In pioneer evangelism the baptism of converts is naturally the norm. This implies conscious decision on the part of the baptised, whatever views the evangelist may hold on infant or adult baptism. This has led in the twentieth century to serious reconsideration of the meaning, purpose and effect of baptism, especially in its relationship to initial confession of faith. Adult (believers) baptism has come into its own. But then so has confirmation! In most paedobaptist denominations the importance attached to these two as a single rite of initiation bears eloquent witness to this development.

The recently published Roman Catholic *Adult Catechumenate* provides a striking illustration. At first sight it looks surprisingly 'Protestant' with its emphasis on instruction, faith and discipleship. In fact, it draws much of its material from the fifth century. It clarifies the connection between baptism and confirmation, and quietly buries the fiction that an infant can be addressed as a believing adult. The 1972 order goes so far as to describe the baptism of adults as 'the norm'. Yet this raised so many problems that in 1980 the Congregation for the Doctrine of Faith had to publish a warning that 'norm' does not mean 'normal'![1]

This has proved to be a common problem in most paedobaptist denominations, where the emotional and theological commitment is still to infant baptism. Baptists have proved a little over-optimistic in their sense that the argument was going all their way, and that 'in a secular and multicultural society ... the normal mode of baptism will soon be as it once was in the early days of the Church'.[2] The glum fact (for the Baptist) is that the infant rite, with its presuppositions, is still built into the system. The adult rite may indeed have become 'the theological norm', but it has not become the denominational normal!

Pathways to unity
A second great ecclesiastical feature of the century has been the growth of Ecumenism. The word (from the Greek *oikumene*, meaning 'all one') is normally employed to describe a pursuit of organized Christian unity. The World Council of Churches, formed in 1946, is its most vocal expression. Reactions to it are mixed, to put it mildly. At one extreme are those who see the goal of the exercise as the fulfilment of

Christ's prayer 'that they may all be one' (John 17:20-21). It is, they believe, an evangelistic priority. At the other end of the spectrum are those who deeply suspect a compromise of non-negotiable truths. At one time their worst fears seemed justified, when the World Council of Churches spoke in sinister Orwellian tones of a united organization chaired by the Pope, with 1984 as one possible target date!

For different but equally obvious reasons, it is the Catholic and conservative evangelical wings of Christendom which have been most cautious about church unity, and the liberal elements which have embraced it with vigour. Nevertheless, across the whole spectrum of church life there has been an increasing willingness to listen to one another in an atmosphere that contrasts with the blinkered bitterness of previous centuries, when vituperation was taken as a measure of spirituality.

The search for understanding has taken a double track. Under the auspices of the WCC, commissions and conferences have examined every issue. Meanwhile some denominations have organized what the business world would call mergers (or even takeovers!). In 1972, the majority of English Presbyterians and Congregationalists came together as the United Reformed Church. The smaller Churches of Christ joined them seven years later, thus uniting one baptist and two paedobaptist groups. Various conscience clauses attempted to resolve the 'rebaptism' problem. Anyone requesting this was to be counselled as to the value of confirmation. If he or she persisted, senior clergy were empowered to deal with each case on a personal-pastoral basis.

In the event, difficulties have arisen from an unexpected quarter. Previously paedobaptist ministers sometimes come to a change of conviction, usually through the influence of evangelicalism or charismatic renewal. They then cheerfully invoke a conscience clause devised for a different purpose, and actively promote 'rebaptism'. More recent legislation has theoretically outlawed this practice, but it still continues.

In the Third World, where Christian leaders are more acutely conscious of the evangelistic imperative, and more than a little suspicious of imported Western divisions, large-scale mergers are more common. The Church of North India and Pakistan was the first to link Baptists with Anglicans, Methodists and Presbyterians. The architects of the new denomination laboured earnestly and wordily to square the baptismal circle. In its 1974 Order of Confirmation, that rite is designed to follow adult baptism (immediately) or infant baptism (eventually). There is a robust public and personal acceptance of God's saving offer, accompanied by the laying-on of hands for an 'increasing experience' of grace and power from the Holy Spirit. The service is set in the context of an evangelistic appeal for others to follow the example set.[3]

In Britain, different routes have been followed after early disappointments. Local churches have found various ways to combine their witness and worship. Some simply share one building at different times. More significantly, others have entered into local 'covenants', with mutual recognition of ministry, and united worship. 'Areas of Ecumenical Experiment' have been launched, more recently dubbed 'Ecumenical Projects' or simply 'Churches Together'. Often, complicated rules allow separate denominational identities to remain within a single congregation. One united Church of England/Baptist church, St. Thomas', Crookes, in Sheffield, allows members either to baptize their children or to dedicate them in Baptist fashion. As they grow and express conscious faith, baptised children may be rebaptized at their own request provided they have not been confirmed. Dedicated children are baptized and confirmed at the same time, often by immersion. In this rich variety, official denominational support is sometimes nervous, sometimes enthusiastic. Always, Christians have discovered each other in shared evangelistic and social concern.

Within this whirl of dialogue and common action, reconsideration of baptism is inevitable. The subject has never been more anxiously explored and more vigorously debated since the Reformation. New definitions are suggested, new rites drafted, new compromises floated, new theologies proposed, and new alliances formed.

In 1982, the Faith and Order document *Baptism, Eucharist and Ministry (BEM)* was received by the World Council of Churches in Lima, South America. In this, theologians of every denomination defined the essential elements of initiation. In one crucial paragraph they were listed as '... the reading of scriptures relating to baptism, an invocation of the Holy Spirit, a renunciation of evil, a profession of faith in Christ and in the Holy Trinity, the use of water, a declaration that the persons baptized have acquired a new identity as sons and daughters of God, and as members of the Church, called to be witnesses of the Gospel'.[4]

This represented theological reflection at its ecumenical best. It made no pretence to offer a basis of agreed practice. The document simply presents the nature of baptismal agreement and disagreement, in an eirenic spirit. Indiscriminate infant baptism is deprecated. The problems and pains of 'rebaptism' are examined, and there is a strong plea for baptist churches to give it up altogether.

In the event, the 'Lima Solution' provided no solution at all. Disappointed, the 1993 Fifth World Council on Faith and Order held in Spain called for churches to work harder at ways to reach agreement. All denominations were again invited to declare that 'infant and adult baptism are equal and valid ways of expressing the combination of faith and divine grace, appropriate to different points of growth'.[5] Once again baptist groups were called on to abandon 'rebaptism'.

English and Welsh Baptists in particular have made a measured and generally sympathetic response. Under the pressure of local 'Ecumenical Projects' and 'Churches Together' schemes, the Baptist Union has agreed 'concordats', first with the Methodist and then with the United Reformed churches. In locally 'united' churches, it is agreed that members or converts asking for believers' baptism after already having received baptism as infants, should first be counselled to accept a public 'renewal of baptismal vows'. If they persist in their request as a matter of obedience to God, they may then be baptized as believers, provided that their membership is then transferred to the membership roll of the Baptist constituent in the local unity scheme.

Nevertheless, the denomination can find no way to agree to the Lima Formula. In a 1996 discussion document addressed to their own people, members of the Doctrine and Worship Committee resisted any abandonment of 'rebaptism', and with marked reluctance rejected Lima's invitation to apply phrases like 'provisional baptism' and 'derived baptism' to the christening of babies. 'The infant rite cannot be truly regarded as baptism, because not enough of the New Testament understanding of baptism can be applied to it. It follows that, strictly speaking we are not re-baptizing ... There are significant elements of believers' baptism missing in infant baptism. Whether or not this makes infant baptism a less adequate kind of baptism, it clearly makes it a different kind of baptism, emphasising a different balance of gospel truths.'[6]

Charismatic renewal

This last phrase, 'a different balance of gospel truths', provides a curious bridge to the third subject of this chapter. For striking as were the evangelistic and ecumenical advances of this century, another movement was at work which produced further change and challenge. The Charismatic Movement explored a different kind of unity, gave a different shape to mission, and indeed offered 'a different balance of gospel truths'. Significantly, its key phrase was 'baptism in the Spirit'.

In the last few hours of the nineteenth century, some American Christians from a fundamentalist-Methodist-Holiness background earnestly sought and discovered the New Testament 'gift of tongues'. Within two years tongues were being spoken in Britain in nightly impromptu prayer-meetings at an Anglican church in Sunderland. Within two decades, a worldwide Pentecostal movement had spawned several organizations, sects and fully fledged denominations. The best known in Britain are the Elim Pentecostal Church and the Assemblies of God. They majored on crisis-conversion, informal and emotional worship, an experience of 'baptism in the Spirit' marked by speaking in tongues, and a belief that the supernatural *charismata* listed by Paul in his First Letter to the Corinthians are available today. Mission activity in Africa and South America has proved particularly fruitful.

Almost exactly at the midpoint of the twentieth century, a 'second wave' of renewal began, first, significantly, in an American Episcopalian church and a London Anglican church. This time the movement remained largely within the main-line denominations. Anglican influence helped to steer the emphasis away from the revivalist anti-establishment and second-blessing characteristics of the earlier wave. Soon Baptists were caught up in what became known as Charismatic Renewal. Other Nonconformists followed more tardily. Then, to the bewilderment of some Protestants, the Roman Catholic Church was affected, with nuns, monks, priests, lay folk and at least one Cardinal enthused. By 1985 the experience was widespread and pervasive, if difficult to define or theologize. A Catholic friend of renewal has suggested that 'the sheer magnitude and diversity involved beggars the imagination ... [Charismatic Christians] make up twenty-one percent of organised global Christianity ... [and] one quarter of the world's full-time Christian workers'.[7]

Charismatics stress the physical and emotional elements in worship: clapping, embracing, raising arms and hands in prayer, dancing, joy, tears, laughter. They produce hundreds of new hymns and songs, to chords and rhythms not previously associated with worship. Further 'waves' have majored on healing, 'signs and wonders', community living, 'deliverance ministries' and most recently the much-debated Toronto Blessing. Charismatics value immediacy and experience almost above all else. They ask not only 'Is it true?' but 'Is it happening?'– and are sometimes in danger of assuming that if it happens, it must be true.

Water and Spirit

Charismatic Renewal was bound to refuel the baptismal debate. A movement that gives priority to experience will demand some kind of correlation between rite, feeling and reality. A movement that glories in physical expression will inevitably pose questions about physical sacraments. A movement that takes the promise, 'I baptize you with water ... he will baptize you with the Holy Spirit' (Matt. 3:11), cannot but explore the links between those two baptisms. So renewal has led to rethinking about baptism.

Some Charismatic leaders are still firmly committed to the older classical Pentecostal view of two-stage blessing, based on selected incidents from the Acts of the Apostles. To them, the normal experience (even the required experience) is a moment of conversion by faith in Christ (the more sudden the better) followed by a separate and distinct infilling of the Holy Spirit (the more spectacular the better). The first imparts the forgiveness of sins, and is marked by conscious inward assurance. The second imparts power for witnessing and service, and is always or often marked by the 'initial sign' of speaking in tongues. This second experience is the Baptism in the Holy Spirit foretold by John the Baptist, promised by the Son of God, and first experienced on the Day of Pentecost (Matt. 3:1-12; Acts 1:1-8 and Acts 2:1-12).

Most Pentecostal denominations are baptist. To them, washing in water finds its obvious chronological place between conversion and Spirit-baptism. It bears witness to the former, as a purely symbolic rite that offers splendid opportunity for confession with the lips as well as belief with the heart (Rom. 10:9). It points forward to the latter, as the happy coincidence of words suggests, paving the way from promise to expectation. In the older Pentecostalism, the second baptism was actively sought and awaited in prayer ('tarrying' as in the Authorized Version rendering of Acts 1:4, 'tarry in Jerusalem for the gift my Father promised'). A later development was the laying on of hands to impart or encourage the reception of the blessing.[8]

Baptism (like communion) is seen in a very Zwinglian light, as 'mere symbol'. Its administration is by immersion and (of course) is for believers only. Arguments for an infant rite are rarely considered, or are rejected with derision. The whole sense of 'something happening' is located in the exercise of faith. You trust God for conversion and then feel it; you trust him for his Spirit and then experience him!

Many of the new generation of charismatics, in contrast, have abandoned (or never held) the classic Pentecostal two-stage understanding. They see their experience in a variety of ways: a discovery and release of spiritual gifts, a renewal of faith as expectancy, a subjective experience of a work of God previously known only at the objective level of promise-and-faith. Others speak of emotional healing, the abandonment of crippling doubt, or the glimpsing of new horizons.

The meaning of sacrament
One consequence of renewal has been a quickened interest in the sacraments. This is not surprising, for charismatics have rediscovered the visual, the emotional and the tactile. The idea of God making himself present 'in' the elements he has created is not difficult in such a *milieu*. Is it pure coincidence that the Toronto Blessing, like the rite of confirmation, involves a laying-on of hands and the ancient invitation, 'Come Holy Spirit'? Is it accidental that charismatic influence is seen in revised communion liturgies? The video programmes *Saints Alive* and *Alpha* have virtually replaced preparation for confirmation in some parish churches and include the laying-on of hands at a point which makes some wonder whether the rite itself has been replaced! In fact it has not, but the rite has been given new meaning and intensity. In some Church of England dioceses confirmation candidates are 'falling down in the Spirit' as the Bishop lays his hands on their heads and prays, 'Confirm, O Lord, your servant with your Holy Spirit'! Encounter with God, felt and manifested, felt in the emotion of a soaring spirit, felt in participation in the sacraments, manifested in visible supernatural events; that is what really interests the charismatic. Explanation and analysis can follow, if there is time and opportunity!

Thus Canon Michael Green, usually regarded as at least a friend of renewal, can vigorously defend infant baptism from an evangelical viewpoint, but with an enriched expectation of eventful initiation. He argues that the Roman Catholic emphasis on the visible church (entered by the visible sacrament of baptism), and the Protestant emphasis on the company of believing people (entered by personal faith), need to be matched by the Pentecostal emphasis on the community of the Spirit (characterized by vivid supernatural experience). He recalls how all three strands are easily identified in the New Testament, and all three have repeatedly re-emerged in the church's history. 'In a truly Biblical theology, Christian initiation consists quite simply of three actions which belong together, though they may be widely separated in time and may be received in any order. They are repentance and faith by the individual, water baptism by the Church, and the giving of the Holy Spirit by God.'[9] The order does not matter (he seems to be saying), as long as something eventually happens!

Baptists think again

Some adult Baptists, too, have seen in charismatic experience a welcome resolution of the traditional tension between 'sign' and 'sacrament'. Some Baptist scholars have always conceded that New Testament references to baptism speak in terms of effectiveness rather than mere symbolism. They have found new support and immediacy from contemporary charismatic experience – an experience which is often described in the New Testament as proceeding from grace alone, expressed by faith alone, yet accompanying baptism and the laying-on of hands.

Baptists give priority to mission and to the local church. Their thinking is best traced in what they actually do and say 'on the ground', rather than in their infrequent theological statements. At this level, a move towards both a charismatic and a sacramental emphasis has taken place, and the two are interconnected.

Stephen Gaukroger, senior pastor of two successive fast-growing churches, is a well-known preacher and writer, and has served as President of the Baptist Union of Great Britain. His little book, *Being Baptised*, intended for baptismal candidates, makes significant and sometimes starling reading.[10]

The candidate is advised to prepare for the event: find a spiritual director with whom progress can be monitored, fast, study the Bible, read solid Christian books, and keep a private spiritual journal; advice that must sound oddly 'Catholic' to many older Baptists. In a chapter significantly headed *Encountering God in Baptism*, the writer counsels, 'Expect God to bless you ... expect to be filled with the Spirit ... don't be surprised if there are spiritual manifestations.' He suggests examples of what may happen: a sense of stillness, tears, shaking, laughter, tongues, emotions, discovery of a new spiritual gift. He recommends the laying-on of hands to accompany or follow the baptism. So 'confirmation' finds a place in the baptismal rite! Suddenly he sounds charismatic rather than Catholic!

Estimates suggest that fifty per cent of English Baptist ministers, and seventy per cent of new ordinands are 'charismatic', and few of them would find difficulty with this approach. It is all a far cry from the kind of advice sometimes given to baptismal candidates thirty years ago: 'Don't expect anything to happen!'

Restoration ... The New Radicals

There is yet another charismatic phenomenon to consider: the advent of the New Churches. The 'house-church movement', as it was originally called, burst on the British church scene in the mid-seventies. With it came a whole new vocabulary of technical religious terms: celebration, heavy shepherding, covering, apostolic ministry, prophetic input, networking, and so on. New crypto-denominational groupings quickly emerged: Pioneer Churches, New Frontiers International, Kingdom People, Ichthus, Covenant Churches, New Life, Salt-and-Light, Community Church; the list still grows.

At first dependent on transfers from the main-line denominations, the new churches soon began to evangelize un-churched people. In 1980s Britain they offered the most dramatic example of growth in an otherwise shrinking Christian constituency. Enthusiastic, brash, visionary, aggressively evangelistic, and operating in frequently-changing alliances, they were to some observers indistinguishable from 'ordinary' charismatics in their emphasis on vivid experiences, spiritual gifts, faith-expectancy and exuberant worship. However, the founders of the new movement would not agree with that diagnosis. Whereas Renewal saw itself as a rediscovery of the life already potentially present in the churches, Restoration saw itself as a root-and-branch revolution that tore off the restraints of tradition and offered to lead the church into the dawning of a new day. Charismatic *Glasnost* must be supplemented with Restoration *Perestroika*!

Restoration was from the beginning visionary, disruptive, innovative and separatist. This 'largest and most significant religious formation to emerge in Great Britain for over half a century'[11] ran parallel with Renewal for the first ten years. It emerged as a distinct movement at the very time when charismatics, finding increasing acceptance in their previously suspicious denominations, opted for staying inside.

This modern movement is the latest manifestation of that orthodox radicalism which has constantly re-appeared in the long history of Christendom (orthodox, because it holds to the great historic truths of Scripture; radical because it deals ruthlessly with what it sees as parasitic growth in the original body). As such, it can be compared instructively with the Medieval Underground, the Anabaptist Movement, the Quakers, the Salvation Army, and the early Brethren.

The new radicals believe that God is doing something entirely new, making his church glorious for the return of Christ. In a little book entitled *Church Adrift*, David Matthews, one of the early Harvesttime leaders, sketched a disarmingly simple view of Christian history.[12] After the death of the apostles, the church quickly lost its way, slipping into an institutionalised and hierarchical Catholicism which stifled its life and compromised its witness. But God has repeatedly recalled his people to the original vision. Successive movements amongst Lutherans, Presbyterians, Baptists, Moravians, Methodists, Brethren, Salvation Army, Pentecostals, and charismatics have rediscovered lost truths, like justification by faith, believers' baptism, the indwelling Spirit, and so on. Now Restoration has come; herald of the return of Christ to a purified Church.

In this view, the 'structures' of Christendom are not merely cumbersome and decrepit; they are actively hostile, expressions of the 'principalities and powers' that repeatedly corrupt even mankind's best endeavours. Many Christians are trapped in denominationalism, shackled by tradition, their worship stunted by formalism. But as enlightened and empowered believers learn to engage the resources of the Spirit, deception will be broken, and Christians will join a mass exodus from formalized, traditional Christianity. That was the theory.

In the event, there has been a flow in both directions. Significant numbers (including clergy) did leave the established denominations, attracted by this radical diagnosis. Some were Anglicans, but many were already Nonconformists, especially Baptists, Independent Evangelicals and (most of all) Brethren.

But the traffic moved the other way too. After the honeymoon period, an unrecorded number of Restoration members, including several leaders, moved back into Anglican or Baptist circles. Distaste for admitted excesses and nostalgia for lost emphases on preaching or order have contributed to this. Meanwhile, many main-line charismatic churches have proved able to adopt significant Restoration insights, given sufficient time.

Nowadays, the gradual abandonment of extreme or overstated positions on both 'sides' has led to a hearty and healthy combining of erstwhile rivals against the real enemies of secularism, paganism and unbelief. Several of the Restoration networks now actively promote friendship, co-operation and even alliance with older churches once regarded as hopeless and hostile.

Restoration and Baptism

This whirlpool of spiritual energy has led to a rethinking of baptismal practice. Baptism in the Spirit (variously understood) is a priority for Restorationists as much as for charismatics, and to both the very word *baptism* demands attention. Christians abandoning the older paedo-baptist denominations found it easy to abandon their initiation rites too. But most early house-church leaders were already baptist in conviction, and saw no reason to change. They simply added the desirability of emotional and supernatural experience to the virtue of baptismal faith.

The pioneers were too busy with other priorities to work out any detailed theology, let alone to write books or produce formal statements. Andrew Walker, their first 'outside' historian, commented that he found only two small books on the subject, both of which dismissed infant baptism in a robust manner, and presented a simple 'this is what they did' argument from the Acts of the Apostles.[13] Of Arthur Wallis, widely regarded as the godfather of the British Restoration movement, Walker says, 'He was never neutral on doctrinal issues, and he was never at ease with those Anglican and Catholic charismatics who seemed quite happy with infant baptism.'[14] This was not due simply to inherited Brethrenism. Wallis's view of the failure of the organized churches made inevitable an advocacy of a church of committed disciples, and therefore of believers' baptism. To be radical is to be aggressively baptist.

More than that, although vivid personal experience of Spirit-baptism is a vital feature of Restorationism, its really distinctive feature is its corporate view of the Christian life. Church and kingdom are at its heart. Its rationale of baptism hangs on more than 'I believe and therefore I am baptised'. Its basic confession could be paraphrased like this: God has called us into his rule of liberating love. He is restoring his church in works of power, lives of goodness and communities of grace. Water baptism is the sign of that calling, new birth is its means, Baptism in the Spirit is its dynamic.

The spokespeople for the New Churches often take as their model the Acts 2 Pentecost-experience, with its immediate consequences as Luke describes them (Acts 2:28-43). It is an essentially corporate vision, within which baptism and Spirit are linked with divinely-motivated community life (1 Cor. 13–14 and Eph. 4).

Not surprisingly, then, Restorationists often view believers' baptism (or rebaptism) very much like the medieval Waldensians and the Reformation Anabaptists. Here is an eloquent protest against the sacraments of a Christendom, bound in tradition and formalism; a Christendom which confuses the kingdoms of this world with the kingdom of Christ. Here is a repetition of one of the oldest arguments against infant baptism, finding expression in a radically new movement.

References

1. A. Kavenagh, *The Rite for the Initiation of Adults; The shape of Baptism* (Pastoralis Actio, 1980).
2. Paul S. Fiddes, (ed.), *Introduction to Reflections on the Water*, a series of essays by British Baptist theologians (Regents Park College, Oxford, 1996), p. 1.
3. *Plan of Church Unity in Pakistan and North India* (Christian Literature Society, 1965). See esp. page 7
4. *Baptism, Eucharist and Mission (BEM)*, Faith and Order paper number 111 (WCC, Geneva, 1982).
5. *BEM*, Notes 12, 14 and 20.
6. *Believing and Being Baptised. Baptism, So-called Re-baptism and Children.* A discussion document from the doctrine and worship committee of the Baptist Union of Great Britain and Ireland (BU Publications, London, 1996).
7. Peter Hocken, *The Glory and the Shame* (Eagle, 1995), p. 14.
8. Clifford Hill *et. al.*, *Blessing The Church* (Eagle, 1995), ch. 4.
9. Michael Green, *I Believe In The Holy Spirit* (Hodder & Stoughton, 1974), p. 216, italics ours.

10. Stephen Gaukroger, *Being Baptized* (Marshal-Pickering, 1992).

11. Andrew Walker, *Restoring The Kingdom* (Hodder & Stoughton, 1995), p. 20.

12. David Matthews, *Church Adrift: Where in the World Are We Going?* (Marshall-Pickering, 1985) p. 21. The book originally appeared as a series of articles in *Restoration* magazine, 1984

13. The two books were, Arthur Wallis, *The Radical Christian* (Kingsway, 1981) and Eileen Vincent, *Something's Happening* (Marshalls, 1984).

14. Walker, *op.cit.,* p. 42.

Part 3

Baptism Today and Tomorrow

12

Problems for Paedobaptists

On the Day of Pentecost, preaching the first Christian sermon, filled with the Holy Spirit, the apostle Peter was stopped in his tracks. Stung by his assertion that they had crucified the one whom God had made both Lord and Christ, the crowd cried, 'What shall we do?' Two thousand years later we are still arguing over Peter's reply: 'Repent, and be baptized ... For the promise is to you and to your children ...' (Acts 2:38, 39).

A great gulf can separate theological understanding and pastoral practice. We may be fully persuaded of the need to baptize those who believe in Jesus (and their children?). We may think we understand the reasons why we do it, and the theological significance of the rite. But applying our understanding to the everyday world of men and women who come to us, for all sorts of different reasons, requesting baptism for themselves (and their children?), may tax our understanding. Indeed, we may find we need to rub some rough edges off the black-and-white theology we hold with conviction. Is God that bothered with theological niceties? Jesus condemned the Pharisees for hanging a yoke round people's necks which was too hard for them to bear!

In the chapters that follow we can write only from where we are now, insular Englishmen at the end of the twentieth century, one a Baptist, the other a Church of England minister. If our concerns are not your concerns, if we misrepresent you where you are at, we humbly apologize.

We have both tried to hone our theological convictions about baptism (which themselves have undergone modification over the years) with pastoral practice in widely different church communities. We are not always completely comfortable with what we do. But we try to hold in creative tension what we believe about Jesus and his command to baptize in the name of the Father, the Son and the Holy Spirit (Matt. 28:19) with Paul's example to become all things to all men, that we might by all means save some (1 Cor. 9:22).

We believe that, whether you are baptist or paedobaptist, you will meet various practical situations which will challenge your theology when you get down to the nitty-gritty of practising baptism. In this chapter we look particularly at problems for paedobaptists.

Baptism in public or in private?

As soon as Christians in the early church believed they should baptize infants to cleanse them from original guilt inherited at birth, they had to baptize *in extremis*. If an infant looked like dying at birth, and many did, it needed to be baptized there and then, to save it from the flames of hell. Thus baptism was allowed in hospital, or at home, or anywhere where an unbaptized infant looked like passing from this world into the next, as well as in church. Among ordinary folk this soon gave the whole practice a superstitious rather than a theological significance. Baptism became not so much the way into the church as the way out of hell, and having the baby 'done' became all-important for reasons which many could not possibly explain.

Furthermore, once baptism moved out of the church, its importance for the church inevitably declined. Church members could not possibly be expected to show true Christian concern for infants whose baptism they had not seen and might not even know about. From being a central rite of admission to the church, baptism began to progress towards the sidelines and its scriptural meaning and importance began to be lost.

Baptism *in extremis* is rightly condemned by modern theologians. Thus Cullmann declares that as baptism signifies entry into the church on earth there is no need to baptize a dying infant as he will not enter the church on earth but will proceed straight to the church in heaven.[1] Nevertheless, old traditions die hard. Hospital chaplains and nurses still baptize dying babies. For many parents who would otherwise rarely darken a church's door, the compelling motive for infant baptism has changed little since the Middle Ages.

But what do you do if distraught parents ask for baptism? For pastoral reasons alone David would never refuse. Then, pastorally, the crisis over, and the sick child hopefully recovered, he would try and teach the parents 'the way of God more accurately' (Acts 18:26). He would encourage them to come to church later, to bring the child for the formal Welcome which is part of his church's baptismal liturgy, and to share with the congregation their gratitude to God for hearing and answering their prayers. And in the years that followed he would try and encourage them to begin to keep the promises they implicitly made on their child's behalf in the emergency baptism.

More common than emergency baptism is the practice of semi-private baptisms in church attended only by the infant's families and friends. In many episcopal churches these are often quite separate from the main services of the week. In non-episcopal churches baptisms are sometimes 'tacked on' to main services. The congregation leaves for home while the parents, family and child may attend only for the baptism.

In either setting, the picture of proud parents, devoid of Christian understanding and making little effort to adhere to Christian moral and ethical standards in their private lives, bringing their new-born babies 'to be done' is no parody, but one repeated all too often in hundreds if not thousands of paedobaptist churches. Huddled round the font in a corner of an empty church, with father's courage suitably fortified beforehand in the public house, they hurry through a few words which mean nothing to them, listen to the assurance 'this child is regenerate', and return triumphantly homewards, the baby 'christened', the mother 'churched', the father relieved that the church roof did not fall in, the neighbours looking forward to eating the christening-cake and 'wetting the baby's head' with further supplies of beer.

Can such a rite as this be called Christian baptism? Surely, if baptism is the way into the church, then it should take place in the presence of the church congregation, not merely on church premises. If paedobaptism involves obligations for the church, then church members should be there. If paedobaptism is to mean anything at all to those who are so baptized, it must constantly be displayed before them, and its significance explained as they grow in the life of the church. As long as baptism remains a hole-in-a-corner affair, this can never be. As long as infant baptisms remain semi-private family occasions, baptists will continue to point in contrast to their own celebrations of the rite when the whole congregation is present, when many remember their own baptism and renew their baptismal vows, when the gospel is proclaimed and when others are often converted by the public witness of the baptismal candidates.

In the Church of England, 'Holy Baptism [of children] is normally administered by the parish priest in the course of public worship on

Sunday.'[2] Good. But here again, pastoral concerns may dictate otherwise. When relatives may wish to travel long distances to attend, a Sunday morning celebration may prove genuinely inconvenient. In some parishes such large numbers of children are still brought to baptism that obedience to the rule would bring baptism into nearly every service. And while congregations will tolerate some disturbance to worship from squawking babies, dignity and reverence are still necessary. So the rule allows baptism to be 'administered at other times' as well. But perhaps all this says something about the general availability of paedobaptism when compared with the number of families who are active and regular in public worship.

Eligibility for paedobaptism

Paedobaptists have always differed on this issue. Some advocate the baptism of as many infants as possible, others urge baptism whenever it is requested, while others contend that baptism should be administered only to the children of obviously Christian parents. In our opinion a scriptural case can be made out only for the last-named position. We sympathize with the view that much of the scandal caused to baptists by paedobaptism is the result of widespread indiscriminate administration of the rite. To say, however, that baptism is only for the children of Christian parents immediately creates a whole series of practical problems.

First, there is the natural problem that Christian ministers find it hard to refuse requests for Christian services even to those who do not regularly worship. After all, they reason, might not the baptismal service itself kindle a spark of interest which, with careful, prayerful follow-up, will one day be fanned into a flame? Cannot the church fulfil its obligations to the baptized child through its prayers and educational programme, even if the parents and sponsors fail in theirs, and might not the sowing of the seed in this way one day bring forth good fruit? A distraught, non-worshipping father came to see David about problems in his marriage. He eventually followed an *Alpha* course and believed. He recalled how he had earlier had his children baptized because, 'I didn't want them to be spiritually lost, as I was!' Would he have ever come if David had refused to baptize?

Added to this are the problems of unpopularity and misunderstanding when baptisms are refused. And in a day when church discipline of all kinds is notoriously lax, what point is there in refusing baptism in one church when parents determined 'to have the baby done' can have it baptized in another?

Secondly, even when a minister decides to restrict baptism to the children of Christian parents, how does he then decide which parents are Christians? Do parents who come to the major festivals and take the church magazine qualify? Is regular attendance Sunday by Sunday sufficient, or should baptism be restricted to the children of parents who come week by week to the communion table? Even answering these questions positively still does not solve the problem. Many still come to church out of obligation yet show little evidence of living faith. Bold would be the minister indeed who would dare to refuse baptism to the children of such as these!

Twenty years ago, when we first published this book, David firmly advocated restricting infant baptism to families where at least one parent was a practising, worshipping Christian. Nine recent years in two country parishes have taught him otherwise. It simply is not worth giving the church a bad image in these communities which such a policy would produce. So he explains the obligations listed in the service, as clearly as possible. The parents should, by prayer, example and teaching, encourage growing children to 'learn to be faithful in public worship and private prayer, to live by trust in God, and come to confirmation'. Through a regular midweek 'Scramblers' service for carers with their pre-school children, through family services, through other children's activities, and through encouraging parents to attend *Alpha* courses in basic Christian understanding, David tries to encourage parents to begin to keep the baptismal promises they make on their children's behalf. Some, in varying degrees, respond. Most do not. But David is persuaded that this pastoral approach to the situation is the only practical one in the Church of England today with its long cultural tradition of indiscriminate paedobaptism.

In April 1997, Archbishop George Carey in a well-trailed sermon pleaded for indiscriminate baptism, and gave his reasons. He maintained that the welcome thus extended to his parents in his infancy began a process that eventually led to their conversion and to his!

There is no final solution to the problem of 'which infants are eligible' for baptism. Colin Buchanan's suggestion that 'the parents are to be living members of the church by communion if the children are to be new-born members of the church by baptism' has much to commend it if only for its corollary that 'communion must take its

rightful place in the life of the church' and become 'the central service of the Sunday'.[3] But this again creates further problems. In Anglican churches where communion has become the central service of
the Sunday, with parents bringing their children to the communion
rail for a blessing, there is now a growing demand for communion for
children before they are confirmed. And this brings us to the next
problem for paedobaptists.

Baptism and confirmation
'If it is proper to administer baptism to infants,' declares reformed
theologian John Murray, 'then the import of baptism must be the same
for infants as for adults. It cannot have one meaning for infants and
another for adults.'[4] Quite so! Yet failure to accept this conclusion in
practical terms has created a situation where there are virtually two
baptisms. Indeed, the Baptist theologian G. R. Beasley-Murray has
pleaded powerfully for a recognition of this fact as a first step towards
the solution of the baptismal controversy.[5]

We showed in chapter four how, historically, confirmation began
when infant baptism became so widespread that it became physically
impossible for bishops to baptize all children in infancy. Thus, parts
of the rite were delayed until the next episcopal visitation. By the
Middle Ages confirmation had become a separate sacrament, although
theologians constantly debated its significance.

While recognising confirmation's lack of scriptural authority, many
of the Reformers retained it in various forms. Today, for some it marks
personal faith and commitment, for others entry into full church membership, for others reception of the Holy Spirit, for others a necessary
prelude to first communion, and for yet others different combinations of all these elements. In the Church of England Alternative Service Book rite, for example, candidates affirm their baptismal promises, and receive the bishop's laying-on of hands with the prayer,
'Confirm, O Lord, your servant with your Holy Spirit.'

At the moment, the ceremony sometimes includes and always precedes first communion, though this is likely to change in the near
future. Because confirmation thus admits candidates to full church
membership there is an ever-present tendency for it to assume greater
importance than baptism itself; indeed, at times, baptism has been
seen as little more than a preparation for confirmation.

Earlier in the twentieth-century Anglo-Catholic writers like Dix and Thornton argued persuasively that confirmation is taught in the New Testament and was always practised in the apostolic church. From verses like 1 Corinthians 12:13 ('For by one Spirit we were all baptized into one body ... and all were made to drink of one Spirit') and Galatians 4:6 ('And because you are sons, God has sent the Spirit of his Son into our hearts, crying "Abba! Father!" '), Thornton detected a distinction between baptism in water, whereby we become sons of God, and baptism in the Spirit, whereby our sonship is confirmed. This distinction, he contended, is given practical expression in the account of the conversion of the Samaritans in Acts 8 who, it will be recalled, were first baptized in water when they believed, and then were confirmed and received the Holy Spirit with the laying-on of hands by Peter and John. Thornton found further support for his position in the distinction drawn by the writer to the Hebrews between 'ablutions' (i.e. baptism) and 'the laying on of hands' (6:2) (i.e. confirmation) and by the significance attached to the anointing of the Spirit (again understood as confirmation) in 1 John 2:20-27.[6]

Dix found further support for this view from his examination of the baptismal rite as described in the Apostolic tradition of Hippolytus. This theologian, it will be recalled, wrote in Rome at the turn of the second and third centuries. He described a complex initiation rite which included anointing and laying-on of hands, besides immersion in water. Here was evidence for Dix that the early church recognized a clear distinction between salvation (as signified by immersion) and the reception of the Spirit (signified by anointing and laying-on of hands). The two elements were normally celebrated together but could take place quite separately as the Samaritan example shows.

Fundamental to Dix's position was his assertion that the *Apostolic tradition* of Hippolytus is not merely descriptive of baptismal practice in Rome at the end of the second century, but, as its name implies, reflects the practice of the apostles themselves. Liturgy changes slowly, Dix contended, and Hippolytus was thus not describing new developments but long-established customs amply demonstrating that the apostles recognized the difference between baptism and confirmation and embodied it in their services in the church.[7]

So ran the argument, though it was quickly challenged by G. W. H. Lampe. He insisted that Dix had placed too much importance on Hippolytus. He denied that confirmation was to be found in the New Testament, and he tended to support the traditional view that once paedobaptism had become established, confirmation was necessary to mark conversion and entry into full membership of the church.[8]

In 1971 the Ely Report concluded that baptism is the one rite of initiation into the Christian church.[9] It went on to recommend alterations in the Confirmation Service to remove the idea that it marks the reception of the Holy Spirit in the baptized.

This radical approach of the Ely Report to the problems presented by confirmation enjoys the support of some evangelical Anglican writers. They have contended that if paedobaptism is true baptism, it must indeed have the same meaning for infants as for adults. Confirmation is thus an unscriptural and irrelevant appendage and must go, to be replaced perhaps by an annual service of ratification of baptismal vows attended by all baptized adults, at which members reaching the age of eighteen would be admitted to the electoral rolls of their churches. At the same time they recommend that baptized infants and children should be admitted to Holy Communion along with their parents, for their baptism, by its very nature, has qualified them for this.[10] In this connection several leading evangelical Anglicans have looked approvingly on the growing practice of Family Communion in the Church of England and at the practice of the Eastern Orthodox churches where baptized infants and children receive communion regularly even while still babes in arms. As we write, the bishops of the Church of England have agreed to prepare proposals which will allow communion before confirmation in certain situations. Confirmation itself will be retained as a rite of adult Christian commitment.

Communion before confirmation opens up a whole new set of issues beyond the scope of this book. Suffice to say that, ever since the fifth century if not before, Western Christians have found it necessary to supplement infant baptism with confirmation, without clear scriptural warrant. Theologically, this supports the view that 'the Baptism of Infants ... cannot bear the whole weight of theological meaning which the New Testament places upon the Initiation of adults'.[11] Pastorally, it demonstrates the need to give those baptized in infancy a public and visible means of declaring faith and commitment to Christ in later years. This pastoral need can run very deep. From time to time every paedobaptist minister is confronted by a youthful and joyous convert to Christ who, perfunctorily baptized in infancy, on reading the New Testament for him or herself wishes to confess faith, not merely in confirmation but in water-baptism, and that usually by immersion! No amount of explanation will persuade them that their infant baptism, ignored by their parents throughout their childhood, was valid. If, for reasons of church discipline, they are refused, they will sometimes find their way to a baptist who will oblige!

The Christian child

This leads to another issue. What is the status of the baptized child in the eyes of God? Even Jesus needed to increase in wisdom and in stature, and in favour with God and man (Luke 2:52). At the very least the baptized infant will need to follow his example, and somewhere along the line will need to make a personal ratification of his or her baptism in personal acceptance of Jesus Christ as Saviour and Lord. John Baillie has grappled brilliantly and lucidly with this problem in *Baptism and Conversion*.[12] He finds the solution in the distinction drawn in Reformed theology between regeneration and conversion. Regeneration is God's act of salvation by grace. Conversion, whether sudden and dramatic, or gradual and quiet, is man's response. At baptism an infant is made regenerate, but later in life he will still need to be converted. This view has its own problems. How these were raised at the time of the Wesleyan Revival has already been shown. But at least Baillie writes with a refreshing understanding of the interaction of theological and pastoral issues and there, for the time being, the matter must rest.

References

1. Oscar Cullmann, *Baptism in the New Testament* (English translation, SCM, 1950), p. 34, footnote 1.
2. *The Alternative Service Book 1980*, p. 241.
3. Colin Buchanan, *Baptismal Discipline* (Grove Books, 1972), p. 17.
4. John Murray, *Christian Baptism* (Presbyterian & Reformed Publishing Co., 1962), p. 48.
5. George R. Beasley-Murray, *Baptism Today and Tomorrow*, ch. 5.
6. L. S. Thornton, *Confirmation: Its Place in the Baptismal Mystery*, (Dacre Press/ A. & C. Black, 1954), *passim*.
7. Dom Gregory Dix, *The Theology of Confirmation in Relation to Baptism* (Dacre Press, 1946), *passim*.
8. G. W. H. Lampe, *The Seal of the Spirit*, ch. 5.
9. *Christian Initiation, Birth and Growth in the Christian Society* (CIO, 1971), ch. 4.

10. C. H. B. Byworth, *Communion, Confirmation and Commitment* (Grove Books, 1972), *passim*.

11. *The Theology of Christian Initiation*, p. 12.

12. John Baillie, *Baptism and Conversion*

13

Problems for Baptists

When we first published this book in 1977, one senior Baptist figure complained to colleagues about the title of this chapter. He stoutly maintained that its words are misleading, since Baptists do not have any problems!

Not many would adopt his position. Indeed, defining baptist belief and practice is a problem in itself! For a start, so many different Christian groups reserve baptism for adults only. They include the Baptist denominations loosely affiliated within the Baptist World Alliance, the even more massively distributed Pentecostal tradition, the Brethren movement, numerous free evangelical groups and thousands of indigenous churches planted in the Third World by the 'faith missions'. To these must now be added the burgeoning 'Restoration' movements in Britain and the USA, with their expanding missionary outreach. Finally, there are complex indigenous movements in Africa and Asia, usually carrying a prophetic or ecstatic flavour, which almost always reject paedobaptism.

Generalizations therefore form the stuff of this chapter. But what universally unites baptist Christians is their insistence that the New Testament so inseparably links baptism with conscious faith that paedobaptism is at best deeply flawed, and perhaps should not be regarded as baptism at all. Naturally enough, those who baptize infants indignantly reject this accusation. Nor have they been slow to challenge the assumption that believers' baptism as actually practised today can be fully and unquestionably equated with New Testament principles.

Baptism and church membership
Since baptism was clearly the means of entry into the New Testament church, most baptists demand it as a precondition for membership. People baptized in infancy and subsequently wishing to join a baptist church (perhaps because of their conversion or spiritual development there) are usually invited to be baptized as believers. This, to say the

least, implicitly devalues or denies their infant baptism. Bitterness and recrimination can result, as the convert becomes a shuttlecock, bounding and rebounding between uncomprehending relatives and indignant clergy.

In fact, some baptist churches are willing to accept people into membership simply 'on confession of faith'. They judge the rebaptism issue to be one of personal conviction, and leave it to the individual conscience. These churches practise what is described as 'open membership'. In contrast, those who insist on baptism after conversion and without exception, are termed 'closed membership'.

Physical problems, like the assumed inability of the very elderly and infirm to be immersed, are sometimes resolved this way too, and a simple verbal confession of faith (perhaps standing beside the pool) is accepted. But this leads to the very odd assumption that the really vital element in baptism is the amount of water used. Either immerse them totally, or leave them completely dry and abandon baptism altogether!

We both recall the heart-searching precipitated in a Sunderland Baptist church of 'closed membership' persuasion, by three successive decisions. First, they welcomed a woman already baptized by sprinkling in the Church of England as an adult believer. Second, they agreed to baptize a frail elderly convert in a wheelchair, by affusion beside the baptistery (though at the last minute the lady herself insisted on immersion, and was lowered into the water, wheelchair and all!). Third, they privately baptized by sprinkling a new convert who was dying and totally bedfast.

Within the mainline English Baptist churches open membership is fairly common, but this is unusual worldwide amongst official Baptists, who normally practise 'closed membership'. The open practice is more common amongst Brethren, Free Evangelicals, and some Restoration groups. Amongst these, believers' baptism is taught as the norm, but not enforced.

A pragmatic reason for apparent casualness in open churches is their commendable reluctance to unchurch people of undoubted Christian faith and practice, simply because they cannot see eye to eye on baptism. A 'closed' approach, they feel, puts baptists in danger of becoming a baptistic sect, rather than a full expression of New Testament church life. Yet the open approach seems to imperil the very witness that Baptist churches in particular are called to make. Recent statistics from the Baptist Union of Great Britain and Ireland cause great concern. Throughout several years of marked evangelistic success and church growth, the numbers actually being baptized continues to decline sharply. This can only mean, ironically, that Baptists are no longer people with distinctive beliefs about baptism!

Baptism and conversion

The whole issue of conversion and initiation presents another area of difficulty for baptists. In the New Testament the administration of baptism is almost or completely synonymous with the declaration, 'I am a Christian.' Peter's command on the Day of Pentecost, the response of the Samaritans to Philip's evangelism, the visit of Ananias to Saul of Tarsus after his Damascus Road experience, the baptism of Cornelius the centurion, Paul's baptism of the gaoler and his family; these incidents all suggest immediacy as strongly as they suggest faith-response (Acts 2:38-41; 8:12; 9:17-18; 10:45-48; 16:30-33 – notice words like 'that day', 'as soon as' and 'at once'). For this reason, some baptists do indeed baptize their converts almost immediately, using the formula 'on your confession of faith ...' They see the rite as that 'confession with the mouth' which, accompanied by 'belief in the heart' conveys and announces salvation (Rom. 10:9).

A more common approach, however, is to lead the converts through an extended course of preparation and teaching, which culminates in baptism 'when they are ready'. Thus evangelism and pastoral care contend with each other on the question 'When to baptize?'

Part of the problem centres round the evangelical mythology of sudden or crisis conversion. This owes a great deal to the Victorian evangelism of the Moody and Sankey variety, but has roots further back in the eighteenth-century Awakening, associated with Whitefield and the Wesleys. 'I know the place where Jesus Christ first revealed himself to me and gave me new birth ... surely it was a day to be had in everlasting remembrance!' wrote Whitefield.[1] 'I was not a Christian till May 24th last,' wrote John Wesley to his brother in 1738, and in a famous diary entry records the place and the precise time in the evening when it happened.[2]

This emphasis on new birth, joyful certainty, heart religion and security in the achievement of Christ on the Cross, has led evangelical Christians, and perhaps baptist Christians in particular, to put great emphasis on 'naming the day'. Since that is not always possible (for many conversions are not in fact sudden), then there is an obvious value in closely associating baptism with this, for everyone can 'name the day' of his or her baptism!

But the fact is that crisis-conversion is only one of several New Testament models for Christian faith and life. Other models include the ideas of journey, pilgrimage, warfare and family life, none of which have the same connotations of crisis-suddenness. Once this is grasped, baptism can be viewed not so much as a crucial moment (which should be as nearly synonymous with conversion as possible) but as one stage on a journey of faith and discovery, one decisive stage in the holy war, one period within the growth of family likeness. In such cases, the best moment for baptism may vary considerably from person to person. The rite is (surely) to be regarded as one point on the journey, rather than a destination.

This approach may help to reconcile different and seemingly contradictory practices amongst baptists, whose very diversity from church to church can easily be derided by those who value uniformity as a sign of clarity. For the New Testament does not only speak of baptism as 'first confession of faith'. See it only as that, and baptists will hesitate to baptize immediately, for fear that the hopeful convert will prove to be disappointing or even apostate (hence the period of preparation and testing). But other New Testament writings urge Christians to look back to their baptism in order to avoid unfaithfulness, or indeed to recall themselves from a lapsed faith (*e.g.* Rom. 6:2-4; Gal. 3:27). As for being 'sure that the convert is ready for baptism', the first evangelists were not sure (can anyone be?), for Philip baptized Simon the magician after he had 'believed', yet shortly afterwards Peter had to rebuke the man as a fraud (Acts 8:9-23).

What baptists struggle with is the relationship of new birth, conversion and initiation. All of these topics may be viewed as crises, but it is equally necessary to view them as processes, or as a 'complex' of many elements, including baptism. To this we shall need to return.

Baptism and children

If baptists find difficulty in administering the rite to believers at the moment of conversion, their problems multiply when they consider the position of children. At what age can children be regarded as believers? What evidence should children offer for the reality of conversion? What is the difference between a child nurtured in a godly home and unable to recall a time when he did not believe, and a child from an unchurched home, influenced by Sunday school, uniformed organization or children's mission, and now wishing to follow Jesus?

Few baptists doubt the exquisite reality of many children's faith. They take seriously Christ's reminder that childlikeness is not a barrier but a passport to the Kingdom of heaven. So if baptism is related to faith, how should children relate to baptism?

Some invoke the useful concept of 'the age of responsibility'. Before that age it is assumed that a child cannot be held responsible for 'unbelief', and is not capable of a clear faith-commitment. But what is this age? Twelve is often assumed, because of Jewish precedents, and the story of the young Jesus in the temple (Luke 2:41-52). But others can recall coming to faith themselves as early as four. One outstandingly evangelistic church known to the authors declines to administer baptism to anyone below eighteen, whilst an American Baptist church with which it has close ties will often baptize children as young as eight!

The latter example is in a context of strongly decision-oriented evangelism, where receiving baptism is practically the equivalent of 'coming forward' in response to an 'appeal'. Most British Baptists are loath to do this. Yet to refuse baptism to a child who earnestly requests it after taking seriously what the preacher has been saying, may cause confusion, discouragement or a sense of rejection.

Christian parents, whatever their view of baptism, teach their children to pray, instruct them in the Scriptures, take them to church, explain the gospel to them, and expose them to Christian teaching and lifestyle. Through all of this, and by the working of the Holy Spirit, they hope to see their children becoming Christians. But if they are Christians, why should they not be baptized? Were the Christian children whom Paul addressed in his letters unbaptized Christians? (see Eph. 5:21-6:9 and Col. 3:18-25).

Most baptists have long recognised this difficulty. One response since Victorian times (resisted by some at first) is the widespread practice of 'infant dedication'. There is no fixed wording for this; various order books offer examples, from which ministers or elders improvise and combine as they wish.[3]

Nor is there a definitive theology behind the practice; baptists do not function that way. But the usual elements, in varied combinations, are thanksgiving (for the gift of life and birth), promise (vows made by the parents and the congregation) and blessing (recalling how Jesus welcomed little children and blessed them). Usually the child is formally 'named' at the same time. The element of dedication is variously understood, either as the dedication of the parents to the task of Christian parenthood or the handing back to God of the infant, that his will might be fulfilled in the child's life.

As well as the need for something to symbolize Christian parenthood and child-rearing, baptists have responded in various ways to the request of the church's neighbours for 'christening', or in some way 'having the baby done'. Understandably reluctant to send the family off to the local vicar, to engage in a ceremony which baptists believe to be at best confusing and at worst false, they cast around for something which they can offer that commends the gospel, and symbolizes God's welcome of children.

Don and David both recall an incident from the time when they served the same newly planted church (the only one of any kind) on a tough north-eastern housing estate. A mother brought her newborn infant, whom she had delivered herself by candlelight during a power-workers' strike. She explained that the baby was not her ex-husband's child, but that of the lodger (now also fled). Her previous children spent much of their time at activities organized by the church, and she 'wanted this one done'. All the previous ones were baptized Catholics, but no-one had any present links with that church.

She made a handsome offer: 'If you do this one, you can undo the others at the same time, and make them all Baptists!' We declined that particular path, but were happy to produce a simple rite for the occasion; one in which the mother claimed nothing more than gratitude for a safe birth (heartfelt indeed!) and the church made the appropriate promises. To have refused would, we felt, have been to deny our pastoral and evangelistic instincts.

The problem is to find biblical precedent for these rites, whether involving Christian or non-Christian parents. Baptists appeal to the example of Hannah, who 'lent Samuel to the Lord', in gratitude for answered prayer for a baby (1 Sam. 1–2, especially 1:11, 22 and 28). This is a fine and moving story, but as precedent for 'dedication' it is a little sketchy. The example did not become a Jewish custom, let alone a Christian command. Moreover, Hannah's gift was with a view to God's service, not in the hope of the child's future salvation, as often expressed in modern dedication services. And of course Samuel was not an infant at the time, but a weaned child at least four years old.

The earlier infant ceremony involving Samuel was something quite different, namely circumcision at the age of eight days. That, of course, was the basis of the baby Jesus' circumcision too, whilst the 'presentation in the temple', described by Luke, was an offering of sacrifices and an act of purification for Mary, not for the child (Luke 2:22-40; cf. Lev. 12:6-8). The other Scriptures referred to are of course the various Gospel narratives in which Jesus welcomed children, blessed them, or drew lessons from their attitudes (Matt. 19:13-15; Mark 10:13-16; Luke 18:15-17).

At best, then, baptists can draw certain principles from the Bible, and offer infant dedication as a helpful means of expressing some of those principles. But in doing so, they risk being teased by paedobaptists, who are accused so often by baptists of doing that very kind of thing with infant baptism! Moreover, infant dedication has become a kind of make-weight to perceived weaknesses in adult-only baptism, rather as confirmation is a make-weight of infant baptism. As confirmation has had to be invented in recognition of the response of faith, so dedication has had to be invented in recognition of God's gracious love which extends to 'children and their children's children ... for ever' (Ezek. 37:25).

In recent years mainline Baptists in particular have given much thought to these issues. In 1966, a statement titled *The Child and the Church* tackled some of them. It precipitated much debate, especially in its suggestion that the child of Christian parents, whilst not a member of the church, is related to it! The statement was 'received but not adopted' by the Baptist Union Council. One of its memorable phrases suggested, 'The infant, regardless of his parentage (is) a member of Adam's race redeemed in Christ. This is not because his parents are Christian but because he is a human being.'[4]

The 1996 report, *Believing and Being Baptised*, with its subtitle *Baptism, so-called Re-baptism, and Children in the Church*, carefully explains the reason why Baptists have devised infant dedication services. It admits that many of the arguments are very similar to those used for infant baptism. It even admits to 'a vague understanding' among many, and that infant dedication 'still needs a great deal of theological reflection and clarification'. But it resolutely defends the Baptist refusal to confuse dedication with baptism. Baptism 'has not been seen as appropriate for young children, partly because of a feeling (often ill-expressed) among Baptists that children are not in the same kind of state before God as a person who has reached an age of responsibility and moral choice.'[5]

Baptists and unity
Finally, Baptists agonize a great deal over their bad image in circles where church unity is earnestly sought. The strong appeal levelled by 'Lima' underlined that again. Baptists struggle on three fronts here. Their deep conviction that Scripture has an authority not possessed by mere 'tradition', allied to their historic defence of conscientious freedom simply will not allow them to forge new arrangements or make new promises that would forbid rebaptism to those who desire it in obedience to Christ.

Moreover, they have no way of entering into such arrangements or promises anyway. Baptists hold to the autonomy or competence of the local church as a central principle. This is not a matter of supposed democracy. As they see it, the attitude springs from a biblical belief in the local 'gathered church' which owes its existence alone to Christ's undertaking to be 'in the midst' of those who gather in his name. No superior church officer exists, and no theologian is authorized to arrange or agree a scheme that squares the circle for all the constituent churches.

To some of these difficulties we shall need to return in our final chapter. Suffice for the moment to say that baptists do indeed have their difficulties. Other Christians owe it to them to understand and sympathize. Equally, the exercise of wrestling with those problems should help baptists to understand the not dissimilar difficulties and issues with which paedobaptists sincerely wrestle. Charity and understanding can only be gain.

References

1. George Whitefield, *Journals*, pp. 57-58.
2. J. Ernest Rattenbury, *The Conversion of the Wesleys – A Critical Study* (London, Epworth Press, first edition, 1938), p. 20.
3. See e.g., Ernest Payne and Geoffrey Winward, *Patterns and Prayers for Christian Worship. 'A Manual for Ministers'* (Carey Press, 1960), and Alec Gilmore, Edward Smalley and Michael Walker, *Praise God – a Collection*

of Resource Materials for Christian Worship (BU London, 1980), and *Patterns and Prayers for Christian Worship*, ed. Baptist Union Department of Ministry (Oxford University Press, 1991).

4. Alec Gilmore (ed.) *The Child and the Church*, 1966, p. 14, a report received but not adopted by the Baptist Union Council. Available from Baptist House, 129 Broadway, Didcot, Oxon, OX11 8XB.

5. *Believing and Being Baptized* (BU Publishing, London, 1966), p. 17.

14

The Real Issues

Our long journey is all but complete. We have attempted to summarize scriptural teaching on baptism. We have looked at different ways of understanding and applying what the Bible says. We have tried to see how baptismal belief and practice have varied during two thousand years of Christian history. Different circumstances at different times have drawn out varying emphases to meet changing pastoral needs and demands. We have also tried to make a careful and constructive critique of paedobaptist and baptist stances as they exist today, looking at their separate strengths and weaknesses. Now we must draw the threads together. We cannot solve the baptismal controversy, but maybe we can understand why Christians defend their corners so passionately.

Baptism and salvation

> For by grace you have been saved through faith; and this is not your own doing, it is the gift of God – not because of works, lest any man should boast (Eph. 2:8-9).

Christian belief has always moved along a spectrum between those at one end who stress God's coming to us before we come to him, and those at the other end who emphasize our response of faith. Sometimes these differences have erupted into open controversy – Augustinians versus Pelagians, Calvinists versus Arminians, followers of George Whitefield against followers of John Wesley!

If baptism is the symbol of entry into the Christian community, these differences of belief will be reflected in baptismal practice. If you are sold on the idea that God comes to us in grace before we begin to turn to him, then the timing of baptism will not be over-important. As a 'sacrament' of grace it can just as easily pre-date faith, and even play its part in the journey to faith, as it can witness to the faith of the new believer.

If a village chief, or even a tribal king, turns from pagan practice to Christ he may well order the rest to obey. Fine! then it is okay to baptize them. Faith will surely follow as Christian instruction and nurture are brought to the rural community or clan. And if a father believes in Jesus, and his wife follows suit, then they will naturally wish to baptize their children. Their infants' baptism will declare their determination to bring them up in the 'discipline and instruction of the Lord' (Eph. 5:4). Their children's baptism will speak of faith incipiently born in their hearts, which will blossom as they grow to maturity.

If, on the other hand, you believe that faith is paramount as evidence of God's loving and searching grace, and if you believe that baptism is essentially the sacrament of faith, then you will wish to wait until faith is declared before baptizing. You will know, from observing others, and from bitter experience, that not all those who are baptized because they 'belong' to someone else – a village chief, a tribal king, a parent – actually come to faith. And you may well feel that if you baptize 'indiscriminately', adults or children, you are spoiling and debasing something that is very precious. Maybe you are making a 'testament of faith' into an empty ritual. Maybe you are giving to those who have been so baptized a false confidence in the mercy of God: because they have been 'done', it matters little what they do. God has accepted them, for good and all.

So, you will forbid baptism altogether to infants who cannot possibly exercise conscious faith. Indeed, you may deny that infant baptism is Christian baptism at all. If infants who have been baptized later come to faith, you will insist on their believers' baptism as a visible sign of God's grace in their lives. As children grow, you will still be cautious when it comes to baptism. Without denying the reality of their belief, you will be aware that it takes a robust and mature faith to withstand the pressures and temptations of adult life. So you may still ask children to wait for baptism, until you have taught them what it means to be a Christian, and until they show clear evidence of serious commitment to Jesus Christ.

Of course, if you are completely honest, you will know that not all who are baptized as believers persevere in following Jesus. Where do they stand before God? How does God regard them? Fears like these caused some Christians in the fourth, fifth and sixth centuries to delay baptism for adults until they knew they were dying, although their example has not been generally followed.

Baptism and the church

If Christian belief moves along a spectrum concerning the nature of salvation, it moves along another spectrum when it comes to the doctrine of the church. When Christians are in a minority in society, and maybe persecuted as well, then the church is quite clearly the community of believers, with the possible inclusion of their children. But if Christians enjoy the support and encouragement of secular authority, if it becomes fashionable to be Christian, and if secular authority welcomes an alliance with religious leaders, then a short step can easily be made to identify the local community, the nation, or even the empire with the church!

This is precisely what happened at the beginning of the fourth century. For three hundred years after Pentecost, Christians struggled with the stigma of illegality. One problem was their refusal to obey the required religion of the Roman Empire, namely to worship the emperor. In successive waves of persecution different emperors tried to enforce the law. Then Constantine became a Christian. But in declaring Christianity a *religio licita*, a legal religion, he did not merely grant Christians freedom to worship without offering devotion to him, but he made Christianity the 'state religion' as well. By the end of the century people were persecuted for refusing to believe! By the end of the fifth century to be Roman was to be Christian. By the end of the fifteenth century the Bishop of Rome was the most powerful political figure on earth!

Inevitably, infant baptism became normal. It still is across large areas of the world where Roman Catholic and Orthodox churches retain strong links with the state. And in northern Europe the idea of 'established religion' survived the Reformation in Protestant Anglicanism, Scottish Presbyterianism and German or Scandinavian Lutheranism. To be born into any of these nations was to be born Christian and therefore to qualify for baptism.

In today's English-speaking world, few would hold to the extreme Christian 'sacralism' we have described earlier in this book. But the idea that the church is somehow larger than the visible body of believers remains strong. Believers' children are obvious candidates for inclusion and therefore for baptism. Where servants are employed they may be too. Baptism, then, becomes a means to faith and not just evidence of it.

At the other end of the spectrum there have always been those who restrict the church to 'gathered communities' of practising believers. Often appalled at what they see as abuse, profligacy and open wickedness in state churches, with their links between bishops and secular rulers, such Christians hold to a simpler and loftier vision. They gain their vision from their perception of apostolic and New Testament Christianity. At this end of the spectrum baptism is quite clearly only for conscious and openly committed believers, for they, and they alone, form the church.

Baptism and sacrament

We deliberately avoided using the word 'sacrament' until we reached the fourth chapter of this book because it does not occur in the Bible. Yet so much of the baptismal debate centres round this word and its meanings.

We showed how the word, used by soldiers to describe their oath of allegiance to the Roman emperor, came to be applied to religious signs of sacred reality. Roman Catholic Christians observe seven sacraments, Protestants two, namely baptism and the eucharist.

Besides being signs of sacred reality, sacraments are also regarded as means of grace. That is, when accompanied by faith, they possess value in themselves. They do not merely symbolize divine realities, but they focus and thus mediate them in some way. Indeed, they may precede faith, encourage it and strengthen it. Christians who receive them will be richer, in some way, than those who do not.

Here again, belief and practice move along a spectrum. At one extreme, and particularly at a popular level, the benefits of the sacrament are stressed, almost to the exclusion of faith. At the other extreme, the importance of faith is stressed, almost to the point of denying any value in the sacrament. At that point, the sacrament becomes an ordinance, observed simply because Christ commanded it. At this extreme, the sacrament/ordinance may become optional or may even be dispensed with altogether.

Very generally speaking, Christians who stress the intrinsic value of the sacrament are more likely to be paedobaptist than baptist. Those who insist on the importance of faith are more likely to be baptist than paedobaptist. The reasons are obvious.

Baptism and covenant

'Covenant' is a foundational concept in the biblical story. God made a covenant with Adam and Eve when he set them in the Garden of Eden. He made another covenant with Noah when he and his family came out of the ark. He made a covenant with Abraham when he called him to leave Ur and settle in Canaan, and he extended this covenant to his descendants for ever. He made a covenant with Israel at Mount Sinai when he rescued his people from Egypt. And he has made a covenant with humanity in Christ at the cross and the empty tomb.

All God's covenants are made in grace. He comes to us before we come to him. We do not deserve his mercy. Covenants are ratified with sacrifice and accompanied by visible signs. With Abraham, the covenant-sign was circumcision. The signs of Christ's covenant are baptism and the eucharist.

The New Testament writers frequently contrast the 'old covenant' made at Sinai (demanding obedience to the Law) with the 'new covenant' in Christ (inviting trustful faith). The first is preparatory, inadequate and imperfect; the second is complete. Nevertheless, behind even the first covenant stands the primary promise made to Abraham, and, by extension, to all who share Abraham's faith.

Since the Reformation, many who follow Calvin's thought have used 'covenant theology' to support a biblical doctrine of infant baptism. They believe this protects vital concepts like the priority of grace and the trustworthiness of God's promises to bless believers and their children.

So is there one covenant, or are there two? Baptismal 'sides' are often taken on the answer to this question. Nor is the question easy to resolve, for biblical writers are not always the systematic theologians some of us would like them to be! In Romans 4, Galatians 3 and Colossians 2, Paul emphasizes the priority of God's covenant of grace with Abraham and the inferiority of the Law, and draws an analogy between circumcision and baptism. In Romans 2, however, the same Paul argues for a purely 'spiritual' circumcision. And in much of Galatians (outside chapter 3) Paul warns of the dire danger of denying God's grace by relying on circumcision! The formula is not, 'baptism parallels circumcision', but 'faith makes circumcision unnecessary'.

In general terms (though with many exceptions), those Christians who value covenant theology are likely to be paedobaptist, while those who find two covenants in Scripture (again with many exceptions) are likely to be baptist. Understanding and respect for differences in balance, emphasis and motives are vital in this whole area.

Children and God

What is children's status with God? Here, perhaps, lies one of the most emotive issues within the baptismal debate.

For Augustine the answer was stark and simple. Since children inherit both sin and guilt through their father's seed, they are bound for eternal damnation until they believe and are baptized. From the moment of birth, baptism is possible so should be administered to wash away sin. Faith should follow whenever possible.

Augustine's prescription became and remains part of the official teaching of the Roman Catholic Church. Many Protestants continue to embrace it, to a greater or lesser degree, and with varying attempts to reword it. It remains an enduring part of folk-religion in Western society, even where virtually every other religious concept has been abandoned.

Christians of Calvinistic persuasion and paedobaptist habit find a more gentle version (devoid of the horrific suggestion that all unbaptized babies are bound for hell) by balancing 'all have sinned' (Rom. 3:23) with 'your children are holy' (1 Cor. 7:14). Children are welcomed within the covenant through their parents' faith. They should be baptized, but God will not withhold his blessing from them if they are not.

For many baptists, insisting on the priority of faith, there is an equal but opposite problem. Should they fear for the eternal security of their children whilst they are too young to believe? Is anyone too young to believe? Is there such a thing as an 'age of responsibility'? This question has legal, as well as moral and spiritual, implications.

There is no clear command for a New Testament infant rite, but may one be produced on grounds of general principle and analogy? And what does Paul mean by 'your children are holy'?

To use a post-modern phrase, traditional beliefs on both sides of this debate are being 'deconstructed' as never before. Will this lead to radical 'reconstruction'? Watch this space!

Conclusion

Many of the real issues in the baptismal debate are concerned with the place of individuals or denominations on a number of different spectra. Few Christians stand at either extreme. Most are somewhere in the middle. Symbol, paradox and antonym are necessary elements in verbalizing God's dealings with humankind, as writers as varied as C. S. Lewis, G. K. Chesterton and James Packer remind us! Different insights need to be held in creative tension rather than destructive competition. Meanwhile, Christians live in a society whose presuppositions and world-view have changed to a phenomenal and radical degree, almost unprecedented in history. Does this offer us a new opportunity to restate the points at issue, to explore them afresh, and even to resolve some of them in a new way?

15

Baptism in a Postmodern World

In the early days of the Russian Revolution, an Orthodox couple brought their infant for baptism. Suitably tanked up with vodka for the awesome occasion, they began to quarrel with the presiding priest who was at least one over the eight himself. So excited did they become that, when the child was accidentally dropped into the font, the mishap went unnoticed for some seconds. Only the action of a sharp-eyed grandmother saved the little boy from drowning. The ceremony then proceeded, and he was duly christened ... Boris Yeltzin!

This true story is replete with interesting baptismal symbolism. We mention it here to underline one point alone. The parents and priest were products of a religious system still largely medieval. The child lived through an era when a totally different system prevailed, and a completely new society was built. It could be described as the apogee of modernism: atheistic, materialistic, secular, scientific, ruthlessly logical. Yet that boy-grown-to-manhood played a decisive part in the collapse and overthrow of Communism, and (as we write) holds the tiller of a ship of state that pursues an erratic and perilous course in to another totally different culture. Now here is a fascinating fact. The only two movements that have continued almost unchanged throughout the fall, and rise, and fall, and rise of three historic cultures are – the Russian Orthodox Church who attach one meaning to Christian baptism, and the Baptist movement that attaches another to that same rite.

The end of this final decade of the twentieth century sees unprecedented change in the cultures and world-views of those societies once called Christian. 'A massive intellectual revolution is taking place that is perhaps as great as that which marked off the modern world from the Middle Ages.'[1] Scholars generally agree that in Western society we are now living in a postmodern world. Every area of life, from moral behaviour to architecture, from politics to television, from religion to artistic expression, is increasingly dominated by postmodernist thought.

The story so far

European thought in antiquity emerged out of animistic superstition and pagan mythology. The lofty idealism and rational enquiry of Socrates, Plato and Aristotle imposed on that world the idea of a single, supreme God as the Source and First Cause of all reality. Into that world came Jesus Christ. Paul's magisterial understanding of his death, resurrection, ascension and imminent return challenged the supremacy of the Roman emperor and the easy morals of a permissive and decadent society.

Constantine's victory in 313, and his subsequent patronage of Christianity, opened the way to the Middle Ages. Christian thinkers, most notably Augustine and Aquinas, interpreted and applied their faith to the world in which they lived. By the end of the fifteenth century the Papacy appeared to rule supreme throughout the continent of Europe. Aquinas harnessed Aristotelian logic to propound a combined philosophy and theology which found reality in one Supreme Being whose law, revealed in the Scriptures and interpreted by the church, was to be the yardstick of human belief and behaviour.

That was the premodern world. Its unity was shattered by the Reformation. Protestants asserted the sovereignty of God and the supremacy and sufficiency of Scripture in matters of belief and behaviour. But the meaning of Scripture became a matter of individual interpretation rather than ecclesiastical regulation. Freed from the shackles of an oppressive priesthood, Protestants engaged not only in theological enquiry but in exploration and discovery of the world around them. Imbued with Aristotelian ideas of God as First Cause, of an ordered world and immutable Laws of Nature, they embarked on a voyage of scientific discovery and exploration which shaped Western civilization. The 'modern' world had arrived, its inauguration variously attributed to Columbus' discovery of America in the sixteenth century, the scientific revolution that began in the seventeenth, and the 'Enlightenment' of the eighteenth! For that reason, modernity is often described as the Post-Enlightenment Age.

The fall of the Bastille in 1789 is sometimes seen as a dramatic symbol of the final end of the premodern period. The Age of Reason and Enlightenment challenged traditional Christian belief in a supernatural God of love who is active in the world and in the lives of his people. Man was the measure of himself, perfectly capable of defining his own beliefs and moral behaviour. Modernism was thus characterized by humanism, rationalism, scientific enquiry, techno-logical advance and, above all, optimism. Descartes' axiom *cogito ergo sum* (I think, therefore I am) was widened into an all-embracing humanistic creed. We have the power; better still, we have the technology! We can do anything with confidence, as long as the right foundation is in place and the right method is pursued. What we do not yet know, we soon shall. The ills of humankind are due to ignorance, not sin, and ignorance can be dealt with through increased education, understanding and inventiveness.

Modernism had its absolutes, but they were not religious absolutes imposed from 'outside'. Rather, they were based on truths universally applicable because they were rationally and scientifically ascertain-able. 'According to the modern world-view, we know what reality is, and we know how to investigate, understand and control it.'[2]

For obvious reasons, modernism had a powerful effect upon Chris-tianity, much, though not all of it, negative. Outside of the church God was first relegated to a distant 'clockmaker' who had created and started the universe, wound it up and left it to its own devices. Then his reality was denied altogether. The Bible was relegated to a bygone age of darkness and superstition, to be regarded at best as an interesting record of humankind's struggle towards enlightenment. Within the church there was a dramatic retreat from beliefs once thought beyond debate. Through 'critical enquiry' God's personal intervention in human affairs in both Old and New Testaments was reduced to myth; the pictorial fancies of later generations fed back into the unascertainable facts of what really happened.

Jesus was seen as human, but not divine; his words and deeds amended, exaggerated and reinterpreted in later centuries to boost the authority of the church. His death was no sacrificial atonement for the sin of the world, but simply a supreme example of self-giving love. His resurrection was not something objective that happened to him, but an attempt to symbolize something subjective that happened to his disciples.

Liberal Christianity sought to accommodate 'the faith once delivered to the saints' to a modernist worldview that swept through Europe, the United States and the rest of the English-speaking world in the late nineteenth and early twentieth centuries. Evangelicals and traditional Catholics stood almost alone in challenging modernist assumptions about reality.

All change again

But other forces were also at work. In two world wars, mustard-gas and the machine-gun, then Belsen, Dresden and Hiroshima, undermined the optimism that modernism spawned. Carnage and suffering, the perversion of science for brutal ends, the seduction of sophisticated people by dark forces of irrationalism and hatred, left many disillusioned about the supposed essential goodness of human nature. The cheerful presuppositions of post-enlightenment thinking were under siege as never before. The author and statesman John Buchan commented ruefully on the verge of World War II: 'The belief in the perfectibility of man, the omnipotence of reason, and the certainty of progress has more or less ended. The inerrancy of science is proving a broken reed ...The world of sense and time has become distressingly insecure, and (they have) no other world.'[3]

At 3.32 pm on 15 July 1972 the Pruitt-Igoe housing development in St Louis, Missouri, was blown up. The development was a pinnacle of multi-storey modernist architecture. Its architects had won prizes for their combination of high technology, modernist aesthetics and functional design. Yet they had produced a project so impersonal and depressing, so crime-ridden and impossible to patrol, it had become uninhabitable.[4] The event has taken on almost mythological significance as a demonstration that modernism was fundamentally flawed. Subtle comparisons with the Tower of Babel seem irresistible. Like its biblical counterpart, the modernist building stands unfinished, its windows broken and its foundations quivering, whilst its builders and would-be occupiers shiver with fear, disappointment and the frightening discovery that they cannot understand each other.

Sixteen years after the destruction of the Missouri housing development, the fall of the Berlin Wall marked the end of Soviet Communism. That system is now perceived to have been the most extreme example of modernism applied to the organization of a vast number of people. The Marxist experiment promised universal happiness and prosperity, based on the inevitability of human progress. It actually brought political oppression, social manipulation and religious persecution on a scale rarely seen since the end of the Roman Empire. Some thinkers date postmodernism from these two events; the destruction of the American building and the breaking down of the Russian wall.

The New Look
The term postmodernism was first applied in literary criticism in the 1950s, then later to architectural styles, and now to a whole philosophy which increasingly undergirds all forms of thought and behaviour throughout the Western world.

From modernist denial of the reality of God, postmodernists move on to now denying the reality of objective truth altogether. Truth is what is true for you, which may be different from what is true for me. Moral values are relative. 'There are no absolutes' is the foundation-statement of postmodernism. The fact that this itself is an absolute statement does not seem to matter! Feelings are now as valuable in discovering truth as reasoned, logical enquiry used to be. The only 'meaning' that a document has is its meaning to a particular reader; to ask what the writer intended, is to ask what is meaningless and irrelevant.

If it feels good then it must be good. If it feels right, it must be right, for me, though not necessarily for anyone else. Reality, in the past, was 'socially constructed' by diverse communities with their own agendae. The postmodernist's task is to 'deconstruct' reality and truth; that is, to disentangle the core fact from the shape it has been given in a particular culture. The typical postmodernist is 'not particularly intolerant of religion, provided that no religion is permitted to talk of universally valid truth'.[5]

Almost every distinctive feature of modernism has been replaced by a postmodern opposite. Pessimism, even *angst*, has replaced optimism. Science may advance technology, but it threatens to destroy the environment, and is a dubious friend at best. Faith in human reason gives way to irrationality and superstition. The emotion of the moment has more validity than the reflection of the past. Morality has no meaning beyond the immediately pragmatic; does it work for me? Image is all-important, for it has the only reality; that of present personal impact.

At the end of the twentieth century we Christians may deny postmodernist affirmations, but we are deeply and half-consciously influenced by them. Notice how important feelings have become in contemporary Christianity, compared with the search for sound doctrine in the 1940s and 50s. Charismatic renewal with its emphasis on spiritual experience and its delight in unstructured immediacy, has great appeal to the postmodernist. The Toronto Blessing has been welcomed by some as the only thing that will convince disillusioned young adults of the reality of God's presence and his forgiving and accepting love. Those who have tried every permissive experience available to them in postmodern culture will be persuaded only by something that is more subjectively overwhelming than all of them put together. Stop trying to understand it, and just enjoy it! The knowledge of God is less important than intimacy with him.

Obviously, postmodernism presents Christians with both opportunity and challenge. Thirty years ago, Christian witness in school and college involved reasoned apologetics that sought to counter intellectual objections to Christianity. Today's young people are willing to consider Christian faith as never before, precisely because materialism is seen to be arid. But they see it as one option among many. Those who come to faith are likely to adopt a *pick n' mix* approach, selecting those areas of faith and behaviour which they like, rather than allowing Christian understanding to challenge and transform their hearts, their intellects and their lives. They make their decision in a world that is essentially pluralistic, whose greatest virtue is that it offers choice.

For example, some postmodern 'Christians' see no contradiction between accepting the reality of God's love, believing in the resurrection of Jesus and looking forward to reincarnation on this planet when they die! Mixing traditional Christian and Hindu thought in this way simply does not bother them. Others will quite happily 'commit their lives to Christ', express their faith publicly in baptism/confirmation, then go and live with a new partner without getting married. (Breaking the Seventh Commandment? But it feels right so it must be right).

If postmodernism is the revolution in Western thought which some proclaim, rather than a passing fad, then twenty-first-century Christianity will be different from anything we have seen before. The church confronts an entirely new situation. The language of thought and instinct has changed.

How might postmodernism affect baptismal belief and practice? We can suggest a number of ways.

Hermeneutics and Biblical Interpretation
Significantly, postmodern thinking began with new ideas of epistemology (the process by which we come to 'know' things), and hermeneutics (the way in which we interpret what we see, hear and

read). In varying degrees, Christian approaches to the documents of our faith (the Scriptures) have been influenced by this. At one extreme are those who empty the Bible of any ascertainable meaning, or any intention of having any meaning. They see it as a fascinating collection of religious beliefs and experiences, but no more. You may deconstruct and then reconstruct its laws, poems, letters and stories in support of what has become 'true' to you, whether that be New Age paganism, Christian liberation theology, the virtue of being gay, thinly disguised Buddhism, feminism, the gospel of prosperity, or whatever appeals to you at the moment.

Yet some postmodern trends have benefited conservative biblical scholars even while they hold firmly to the Bible's inspiration and authority. In the vital task of interpreting and applying the message of the Scriptures to new situations, they can welcome new insights, recognize new questions and learn to handle new tools.[6]

For example, although Christian scholars still recognise that the Bible contains much propositional truth and many absolute statements (something quite unacceptable to postmodernists), they also acknowledge that not all Scripture is cast in that form. Huge tracts of the Bible are occupied with narrative (like Joshua or Luke). Many passages concern themselves with emotion and reaction to circumstances (like Psalms or Job). There are hundreds of signs, symbols, parables and metaphors which need to be interpreted. But narrative, story, emotion, experience, sign and symbol are all categories in which postmodernism is thoroughly at home. The classic Protestant approach has been to construct a systematic theology by ransacking every part of the Bible for 'texts', treating them all as either direct or implied statements of doctrinal truth, and according them equal status and importance, sometimes quite regardless of context. A lot of rethinking in this area now goes on.

For example, the Christian reader is challenged to look again at the baptismal narratives in the New Testament. How are they to be read? Are they really 'about' baptism? Consider Peter's oft-quoted words on the Day of Pentecost (Acts 2:38-41). Is this really a treatise on Christian initiation? What of its Jewish context? What of its place in God's historical action?

The famous story of the Philippian gaoler (Acts 16) certainly includes a baptism, but is that its real purpose? Paul's reference to dying and rising with Christ certainly invokes the baptismal image, but almost incidentally; it is 'about' living a life transformed by God's redeeming grace (Rom 6:1-7) and only incidentally offers clues about the meaning and mode of baptism.

More fundamentally, we might consider the threefold account of Jesus' baptism, plus the curious half-reference, half-interpretation made by John (Matt. 3, Mark 1, Luke 3 and John 1:29-34). Is this really 'about' baptism? Or is its purpose to convey profound truths about Christ's growing self-consciousness as Son of God and Messiah, and the Christian's growing discovery of him as Lord?

Every one of these biblical references cries out for deconstruction: the exercise of unpacking the circumstances that threw up the event, analysing the pressures that produced interpretations of it, then re-applying their fundamental challenge to today's situation. This is what Tertullian was doing with baptismal passages in the second century, when he warned of premature baptism. Cyril of Jerusalem was doing something similar in the fourth century, with his detailed training, his annual mass-baptisms and his elaborate ceremonies involving oil, salt, water, candles and exorcisms. Anabaptists were engaged in the same exercise during the sixteenth century, when they linked baptism with political persecution and martyrdom. How should we handle it today?

The Anglican theologian Tom Wright has likened the Bible 'story' or 'metanarrative' (favourite postmodernist terms) to an unfinished dramatic script. Acts I, II and III of the drama concern Creation, the Fall, and the Story of Israel. Act IV is the story of Jesus, the decisive pivotal action which resolves the plot. Act V is the story of the church, and Act VI reveals the climactic 'End', hinted at in Revelation and elsewhere. But Act V is interrupted and unfinished; there is no clear, detailed and unbroken line from there to the End. Of course not, for the End has not yet come; the church's story still continues to this day, and we are part of it. The actors (ourselves) have in part to improvise an ending to that Act V (or at any rate a continuation of it). Improvise, but not invent. We have the inspired script so far, plus an outline of the divine author's plot intentions. Our improvisation must be consistent with the previous script and the declared intention. But there is room for reverent exploration and improvisation; which, it is suggested, is what we see the early Christians themselves engaged in as we read Acts and the Epistles. [7]

This approach is called Faithful Improvisation. It has obvious dangers, but it offers a fascinating break-through in baptismal debate as well as in many other church issues. It assumes an authoritative Bible, but also admits what is a repeatedly observable fact: that equally committed readers of the Bible can come to different interpretative conclusions in different circumstances, without needing to doubt one another's integrity. They certainly do so when it comes to baptism.

Sacrament, sign and symbol

The Western world with its heritage of Latin logic, has for centuries downgraded the value and power of sign and symbol. Postmodernism, with its (dangerous) distaste for the rational and the verbal, has nevertheless done a service by restoring the value of the visible, symbolic, tangible and sacramental. A modern Baptist makes a striking point: 'Water in baptism is not merely a visual aid to help us understand various spiritual concepts; in its sheer materiality or "stuffness" it actually communicates the presence of the transcendent God. A created thing provides places and opportunities for a transforming encounter.'[8]

One only has to reflect on the rich and varied significance of water today (cleansing, refreshment, life, energy, power, birth, death, communication, fruitfulness) to recognize the eloquence of the baptismal symbol, and how easily symbol becomes sign, and sign becomes sacrament. Half an hour with a Bible concordance will reveal the rich potential of spiritual meaning implicit in words like water, river, stream, pool, fountain and lake. Several modern baptismal liturgies explore the symbolism of the Spirit moving upon the primeval waters, Noah's flood, Israel's crossing of the Red Sea, Naaman's immersion in Jordan, Zechariah's opened fountain and Ezekiel's deepening river.

A postmodern culture can encourage Christians to explore together what we might understand by God's action in baptism – and to do it anew, not in the old context of faith versus religious work, or national solidarity versus separated church, but in the categories crying out to be explored today. What does faith-baptism say, for example, to a society driven, dehumanized and enslaved by impersonal market forces, in which human beings are mere statistics or consumers? What does faith-baptism offer to those who are marginalized for economic, sexual, social or racial reasons, when St Paul says, 'You are all sons of God through faith in Jesus Christ, for all of you who were baptised into Christ have clothed yourselves with Christ ... you are all one in Christ Jesus' (Gal. 3:26-28, NIV)?

We all know that a sign or symbol not only points us in a certain direction; it may well encourage us (or even cause us) to take that direction. It not only says something, but it does something! I may embrace someone because I already feel affectionate; I may equally well feel increasingly affectionate because I embrace! A silent moment on my knees will sometimes be my symbolic response to a sense of God which I already have. Equally, the decision to get on my knees and be silent will sometimes spark a new sense of God's presence in that very action.

The Baptist theologian John Drane recounted a deeply moving experience in the immediate aftermath of the Dunblane massacre of children and their teacher. Standing by the banks of flowers at the school gate, he was approached by some tough teenagers, who were lighting candles with their cigarettes. They recognized him as a minister, and demanded that he 'say some words' (of prayer) for them. He tried, but dissolved in tears. They began to ply him with questions. 'What kind of world is this?' 'Can I dare to trust God?' 'Do I need to change?' One of them then knelt and placed his knife among the flowers, with the words, 'I'll not be needing this now.' Others followed, with a cosh, a bicycle chain and similar crude weapons. John Drane sensed that this was holy ground; that these youths were meeting God in a new way; that a profound act of repentance was taking place, in which symbols spoke louder than words, and had in themselves life-changing power.

This kind of reflection on the power and necessity of symbolism, perhaps as much as an experience of 'renewal', has encouraged an increasing number of Baptists to use robust sacramental language in their discussions of baptism. Says Paul Fiddes, 'Water is a place in the material world that can become a rendezvous with the crucified and risen Christ.' Christopher Ellis maintains, 'Sacramental theology ... is directly linked to the Incarnation of Christ, the embodied nature of discipleship whereby the church is called to live in the world, and the eschatological hope whereby the sacramental use of material things might prefigure the redemption of all things.'[9]

Seen this way, 'grace' is not some kind of supernatural substance that is impartially poured out in certain circumstances, by mechanical means. It is the gracious coming of God as supremely personal into relationships that are symbolized in materials that he has created and we have embraced in faith.

Unity and Understanding

The postmodernist instinctively treats uniformity with suspicion and greets diversity with delight. Does this suggest some way forward for Christians who are tired of the confrontational 'I'm right, you are wrong' approach to baptism? Richard Kidd, Principal of Northern Baptist College in Manchester, obviously thinks so. He proposes a process of 'letting go', that may 'release people to discover meaning in the diversity of baptismal principles and practices, and enable them to celebrate that diversity rather than struggle against it'.[10]

How is that to be done? He proposes what this book has tried to do in its modest way. We should re-examine the cultural, historical and denominational dynamics that have influenced Christians in their differing conclusions about baptism. Then we should analyse today's (often different) pressures, and find newly appropriate emphases. Using typical postmodernist language, he maintains that an 'explanatory framework' could be provided, within which we can start to understand 'why a living cultural text such as baptism takes on a plurality of lives and rightly becomes styled in radically different ways in different cultural contexts'.[11]

It is easy to identify some of today's new 'cultural contexts'. An Anglican priest finds that virtually no-one brings their children for baptism, because they (the parents) are completely pagan. A United Reformed minister sees 'renewal' in his congregation, leading to repeated requests for rebaptism. Bewildered Roman Catholics discover that their newly built chapel has a tiled and stepped baptistery, and their priest is offering an *Alpha* course which features baptism in the Spirit. A fast-growing Baptist church is filled with new converts who have no desire either to be baptized or to become Baptists, but are anxious to build Christian families in which children are counted as Christians.

Further afield, a citizen of Russia discovers to his bewilderment that a free market economy is as productive of greed, poverty, vice, crime and injustice, as a command economy was productive of tyranny, cruelty and drab inhumanity. Where is he to look for a genuinely new society? What might baptism say to him?

One significant feature of our day is the virtual disappearance of 'community'. Baptism, accompanied by gospel proclamation, says: you may become a child of God. Another postmodern feature (perhaps its most distinctive) is pluralism, including religious pluralism.

All 'spiritual' experience and belief is considered equally valid. The baptismal message can only confront this head-on: Jesus is Lord; he has acted uniquely for the world's salvation; turn to him and bury all that denies it.

We need not panic. Both of these factors bring us closer to New Testament conditions than we have been for fifteen hundred years, and last time round, far from perishing, the church won the day.

A fundamental feature of today's culture is the absence of absolutes, the denigration of authority, and the denial of what postmodernists call the metanarrative. This latter phrase connotes the big story which almost all cultures possess and pass on, to explain who we are, why we behave in certain ways, and where we are heading. The most pervasive metanarrative of this century has been the Marxist-Leninist Story, now increasingly abandoned and discredited. The Modernist-Humanist Story expounded the inevitability of human progress. The Jewish Story is found largely in the books of Exodus, Joshua and Isaiah, and clashes before our eyes with the Islamic Story. But for the postmodernist, there is no metanarrative. All we have is a collection of little personal stories; 'my narrative'. That is one reason for the public's apparently insatiable appetite for televized and radio chat-shows, phone-ins, and the like. In the absence of a universal Big Story (an account of how things really are, which is true for all people all the time and in the same way), how splendid it is to hear how different people work out a satisfying story for themselves! And how comforting to know that my way of working it out is as true and valid as anyone else's!

This offers a splendid opportunity for Christians to share their faith. For we, of all people, do indeed have a personal story, often called a testimony. And our neighbours may well be in a mood to listen to it. Much fruitful modern evangelism inside and outside of our churches seeks to exploit this fact. But behind our stories stands the Great Story, and our witness involves the insistence that the Great Story is true. There really is a metanarrative; we call it Scripture!

At the point of personal testimony, the Christian offers postmodern society something that it welcomes. But at the point of gospel proclamation, the Christian confronts and contradicts our society. What we need to explore (together) is the way in which baptism brings together personal story and metanarrative. In baptism we share our personal testimony. 'This is how I found God, and this is how I (and my family?) intend to behave because of that.' But also in baptism we re-affirm in words and symbol the Big Story of Creation, Fall, Incarnation, Crucifixion, Resurrection, Ascension and Holy Spirit, which would still be true in the absolute sense, even were no-one to be found believing it at the moment.

This is why Protestants have insisted that preached word and sacrament must always go together. The more we reach untaught and previously unbelieving people, the more crucial it is that we have a message, a word, a proclamation. Otherwise, ten years from now, we shall have churches happily filled with people who have stories to tell, but who know little of the Big Story, the truth of God.

The evangelistic imperative therefore demands that Christians work together (not in opposition) to interpret gospel and baptism for the people of this age. 'The world is already too racked with pain and conflict to permit Christians the luxury of adding to its fragmentation by internal arguments about baptism,' says Richard Kidd. He continues:

'I can no longer work ... with a stark and uncompromising contrast between believers' baptism, which is right, and infant baptism, which is wrong. Rather, I am discovering here two histories of the one sign we call baptism, both of which are proper responses to social and cultural encounters across the years ... These histories simply cannot be mixed, nor should one be allowed to replace the other; for in both these ways, the proper integrity of each would be destroyed ... But I would like to think that I can participate in and celebrate the integrity of what is other, without threat to what is profoundly my own.'[12]

The collection of essays that includes those words also quotes the touching testimony of a young man, Richard Bowers, who has Down's Syndrome. He was baptized in a London church in March 1990.

'I was baptised four years ago, when I became like a Christian. (Three ministers) were there. I wore special clothes – white shirt and cream trousers and just feet. The water was open. I go down the steps. The minister was preaching. My hands together on my tummy. The minister said, Father Son and Holy Spirit take me, and I was baptised. She tip me over under the water. My brother came into the water and helped me, wrapped me up to keep me warm. I changed my clothes. Afterwards all my family in the porch in the front of the church – my father took photographs. Then we come back down-stairs and everyone helped celebrate of me – with nice cards and presents. I am a member of the church. I like the communion service. I wear a little cross to show I am a Christian.'[13]

In those artless words, the sensitive reader will notice at least sixteen profound statements about the gospel, baptism and church. To a simple believer with childlike faith, the Gospel has become *his story*. He may never understand the complexities of covenant theology nor the reasons for Tertullian's protest against infant baptism. But his baptism has become for him the means to a knowledge of a loving God, and to membership of a caring worldwide family. Of such is the Kingdom of heaven.

References

1. Diogenes Allen, *Christian Belief in a Postmodern World* (Westminster/John Knox Press, 1989), p. 2.
2. J. Richard Middleton and Brian J. Walsh, *Truth Is Stranger Than It Used To Be – Biblical Faith in a Postmodern Age* (SPCK, 1995), p. 20.
3. John Buchan, *Memory Hold-the-Door* (Hodder & Stoughton, 1947), p. 193.
4. See Gene Edward Veith, *Guide to Contemporary Culture* (Crossway Books, 1994), p. 39 and accompanying footnotes.
5. D. A. Carson, *The Gagging Of God* (IVP, 1996), pp. 347-348.
6. See the seminal works by John Goldingay, *Models for Scripture*, and *Models for Interpretation of Scripture* (Paternoster Press, 1994 and 1995).
7. Middleton & Walsh, *op cit*, pp. 181-185.
8. Paul Fiddes (ed.), *Reflections On The Water* (Smyth & Helwys, 1996), p. 58.
9. *Ibid*, pp. 43 and 49-47.
10. *Ibid*, p. 86.
11. *Ibid*, p. 87.
12. *Ibid*, pp. 85 and 96-97.
13. *Ibid*, pp. 17-18.

SCRIPTURE INDEX

INDEX OF NAMES

Lampe, G. W. H. 25, 147
Latourette, Kenneth S. 77, 88,
    123
Lewis, C. S. 27, 166
Livingstone, David 118, 124
Loyola, Ignatius 118
Luther, Martin 39, 50, 70, 71,
    75, 77-80, 83, 84, 85, 86-
    88, 90, 91, 94, 95, 96

Manz, Felix 75
Marcel, Pierre Ch. 31
Marshall, D. W. 88
Matthew, Jan 92
Matthews, David 134
Melanchthon, Philip 80, 88
Middleton, J. Richard 182
Müller, George 120
Murray, John 146

Origen 27, 41, 43, 56, 61, 67
Owen, John 100, 101-103, 105,
    107, 108

Packer, James 166
Phillips, Obbe 93
Plato 168
Polycarp 27, 43

Rattenbury, J. Ernest 158
Rogers, William 100
Robinson, H. Wheeler 74
Ryle, J. C. 114

Simeon, Charles 114
Simons, Menno 88, 90-94, 99
Smyth, John 100
Sockler, Hans 84
Spurgeon, C. H. 42, 52, 122, 123
Stevenson, J. 41, 67
Studd, C. T. 122

Taylor, Hudson 119
Tennant, William 110
Tertullian 43, 55, 56, 60, 66, 67,
    174, 180
Thompson, Andrew 108
Thornton, L. S. 147

Veith, Gene Edward 180
Verduin, Leonard 74, 88, 89
Vincent, Eileen 136

Waldo, Peter 69, 71
Walker, Andrew 135
Wallis, Arthur 135
Watson, Thomas 100, 102, 108
Wesley, Charles 111, 112, 113,
    115, 153
Wesley, John 109, 111, 112,
    113, 153, 160
Whitefield, George 110, 111,
    114, 153, 160
Williams, G. H. 74, 88, 89
Wright, Tom 174

Xavier, Francis 118

Zwingli, Ulrich 75, 80-82, 83, 85

SUBJECT INDEX

Select Bibliography

Aland, Kurt, *Did the Early Church Baptize Infants?*, English translation SCM, 1963.

Allen, Diogenes, *Christian Belief in a Postmodern World*, Westminster/John Knox Press, 1989.

Baillie, John, *Baptism and Conversion* Oxford University Press, 1964.

Bainton, Roland, *Here I Stand*, Lion Publishing, 1983.

Baptism and Confirmation Today, Joint Committees on Baptism, Confirmation and Holy Communion to the Convocations of Canterbury and York, SPCK, 1955.

Baptism, Eucharist and Mission (BEM), Faith and Order paper number 111, World Council of Churches, Geneva, 1982.

Baptist Union Department of Ministry, (ed.), *Patterns and Prayers for Christian Worship*, Oxford University Press, 1991.

Baptists and Unity, Baptist Union of Great Britain and Ireland, 1967.

Baptists for Unity, Baptist Renewal Group, 1969.

Barth, Karl, *The Teaching of the Church Regarding Baptism*, English translation SCM, 1948.

Beasley-Murray, G.R., *Baptism in the New Testament* Macmillan, 1963; reissued Paternoster Press, 1972.

Beasley-Murray, G.R., *Baptism Today and Tomorrow*, Macmillan, 1966.

Believing and Being Baptised: baptism, so-called re-baptism and children in the church. A discussion document from the Doctrine and Worship Committee of the Baptist Union of Great Britain and Ireland, Baptist Union Publications, London, 1996.

Biblical Doctrine of Baptism, study document issued by a Special Commission of the Church of Scotland, 1958.

Brittain, Vera, *In the Steps of John Bunyan* Rich & Cowan, 1950; reissued R. West publishers, 1973.

Broadbent, E.H., *The Pilgrim Church* Pickering & Inglis, 1935.

Buchanan, Colin O., *A Case for Infant Baptism*, Grove Books, 1973.

Buchanan, Colin O., *Baptismal Discipline*, Grove Books, 1972.

Burton, Jeffery, *Dissent and Reform in the Early Middle Ages*, Cambridge University Press, 1968.

Byworth, C. H. B. *Communion, Confirmation and Commitment,* Grove Books, 1972.

Calvin, John, *Institutes of the Christian Religion,* English translation, SCM, 1961.

Carson, D.A., *The Gagging of God,* Inter-Varsity Press, 1996.

Christian Initiation: Birth and Growth in the Christian Society, The Commission on Christian Initiation, commonly known as the Ely Report, Church Information Office, 1971.

Coates, C.A., Letters of, Stow Hill Bible and Tract Depot, undated.

Cook, Henry, *What Baptists Stand For,* Carey Kingsgate Press, 1947.

Cullmann, O., *Baptism in the New Testament,* English translation SCM, 1950.

Dallimore, Arnold, *George Whitefield,* Banner of Truth, 1970.

Dix, Dom Gregory, *The Theology of Confirmation in Relation to Baptism,* Dacre Press, 1946.

Douglas, J.D. (Ed.), *The New International Dictionary of the Christian Church,* Paternoster Press, 1974.

Evans, Ernest, *Tertullian's homily on baptism,* SPCK, 1964.

Farrar, Frederic, *The Life and Work of St. Paul,* Cassell, 1904.

Fiddes, Paul S. (Ed.) with a response by Rowland, Christopher, *Reflections on the Water: understanding God and the world through the baptism of believers,* Smith & Helwys, Georgia, 1996.

Gaukroger, Stephen, *Being Baptized,* Marshall-Pickering, 1992.

Gilmore, A. (Ed.), *The Pattern of the Church: a Baptist view,* Lutterworth, 1963.

Gilmore, Alec, (Ed.), *The Child and the Church,* a report received but not adopted by the Baptist Union Council, 1966. Available from Baptist House, 129 Broadway, Didcot, Oxon, OX11 8XB.

Gilmore, Smalley and Walker, *Praise God: a collection of resource materials for Christian worship,* Baptist Union, 1980.

Goldingay, John, *Models for Interpretation of Scripture,* Paternoster Press, 1995.

Goldingay, John, *Models for Scripture,* Paternoster Press, 1994.

Goold, William, (Ed.), *John Owen: Collected works,* Banner of Truth, 1965.

Green, Michael, *I believe in the Holy Spirit,* Hodder & Stoughton, 1995.

Hill, Clifford *et al., Blessing the Church,* Eagle, Guildford, 1995.

Hocken, Peter, *The Glory and the Shame,* Eagle, Guildford, 1995.

Holland, Bernard G., *Baptism in Early Methodism,* Epworth, 1970.

Jeremias, Joachim, *Infant Baptism in the First Four Centuries,* English translation SCM 1960.

Jeremias, Joachim, *The Origins of Infant Baptism,* English translation SCM 1963.

Jewett, Paul K., *Infant Baptism and Confirmation,* copyright 1960, unpublished.

Jones, Cheslyn (Ed.), *The Study of Liturgy,* SPCK, 1992.

Kavenagh, A., *The Rite for the Initiation of Adults: the Shape of Baptism,* Pastoralis Actio, 1980.

Kelly, J.N.D., *Early Christian Doctrines,* A. & C. Black, second edition, 1960.

Kingdon, David, *Children of Abraham,* Henry E. Walter Ltd., 1973.

Knaake, J.F.K. (Ed.), *The Works of Martin Luther,* Muhlenburg Press for Concordia, 1960.

Lampe, G.W.H., *The Seal of the Spirit,* SPCK, 1967.

Latourette, Kenneth Scott, *A history of the Expansion of Christianity,* Eyre & Spottiswoode, 1954; reissued Paternoster Press, 1971.

Marcel, Pierre Ch., *The Biblical Doctrine of Infant Baptism,* English translation, James Clarke, 1953.

Marshall, D.W. *et al., Approaches to the Reformation of the Church.* Six papers given at the Puritan and Reformed Studies Conference, December 1965, published by *The Evangelical Magazine.*

Matthews, David, *Church Adrift: where in the world are we going?*, Marshall-Pickering, 1985.

Middleton and Walsh, *Truth Is Stranger Than It Used To Be: Biblical Faith in a Postmodern Age,* SPCK, 1995.

Miller, Andrew, *Church History,* G. Morrish, 1874-1879; reissued Pickering & Inglis, 1963.

Murray, John, *Christian Baptism,* Presbyterian & Reformed Publishing Co., 1962.

Offor, George (Ed.), *The Works of John Bunyan,* Blackie & Son, 1848.

Pawson, David & Buchanan, Colin, *Infant baptism Under Cross-examination,* Grove Books, 1974.

Payne, Ernest and Winward, Geoffrey, *Patterns and Prayers for Christian Worship: a manual for ministers,* Carey Press, 1960.

Pocknee, Cyril F., *Water and the Spirit,* Darton, Longman & Todd, 1967.

Rattenbury, J. Ernest, *The Conversion of the Wesleys: a critical study,* Epworth Press, 1938.

Roberts-Thomson, *With Hands Outstretched,* Marshall, Morgan & Scott, 1962.

Robinson, H. Wheeler, *Baptist Principles,* Carey Kingsgate Press, 1935.

Scheme of church union in North India and Pakistan, Christian Literature Society, fourth revised edition, 1965.

Spurgeon, Charles Haddon, *The Early Years: autobiography,* Banner of Truth, 1967.

Stevenson, J. (Ed.), *A New Eusebius,* SPCK, 1960.

Thornton, L.S., *Confirmation: its place in the baptismal mystery,* Dacre Press, 1954.

Veith, Gene Edward, *Guide to Contemporary Culture,* Crossway Books, 1994.

Verduin, Leonard, *The Reformers and Their Stepchildren,* Paternoster Press, 1964.

Vincent, Eileen, *Something's Happening,* Marshall, 1984.

Walker, Andrew, *Restoring the Kingdom,* Hodder & Stoughton, 1995.

Wallis, Arthur, *The Radical Christian,* Kingsway, 1981

Watson, Thomas, *The Ten Commandments,* Banner of Truth, 1962.

What Jewish Mikva'ot can tell us about Christian baptism, Biblical Archaeology Review, Washington DC, January-February 1987.

White, R.E.O., *The Biblical Doctrine of Initiation,* Hodder & Stoughton, 1960.

Williams, G.H., *The Radical Reformation,* Weidenfield & Nicolson, 1962.